LOST

How Educati
Young Workir

Alex Blower

P

First published in Great Britain in 2025 by

Policy Press, an imprint of
Bristol University Press
University of Bristol
1–9 Old Park Hill
Bristol
BS2 8BB
UK
t: +44 (0)117 374 6645
e: bup-info@bristol.ac.uk

Details of international sales and distribution partners are available at
policy.bristoluniversitypress.co.uk

© Bristol University Press 2025

British Library Cataloguing in Publication Data
A catalogue record for this book is available from the British Library

ISBN 978-1-4473-7024-6 hardcover
ISBN 978-1-4473-7025-3 paperback
ISBN 978-1-4473-7026-0 ePub
ISBN 978-1-4473-7027-7 ePdf

The right of Alex Blower to be identified as author of this work has been asserted by
him in accordance with the Copyright, Designs and Patents Act 1988.

Cover design: Lyn Davies
Front cover image: iStock/Ole Schwander
Bristol University Press and Policy Press use environmentally
responsible print partners.
Printed and bound in Great Britain by CPI Group (UK) Ltd,
Croydon, CR0 4YY

Bristol University Press' authorised representative in the
European Union is: Easy Access System Europe,
Mustamäe tee 50, 10621 Tallinn, Estonia,
Email: gpsr.requests@easproject.com

Contents

Acknowledgements

I owe people too many thank yous to count, but the first goes to my mum and dad (or Val and Don if I'm feeling brave!). I am so grateful that you have supported my efforts to write this book and in doing so tell some of our story. Thinking about it all again hasn't always been easy, and I'm eternally grateful that I get to call you my parents.

Secondly, thank you to all the young men who contributed to this book. Not just Jay, Geo and Fear from the 'Learning from the real experts' chapter, but all of you that I have had the privilege of meeting over the last ten years in workshops, youth clubs, school classrooms and lecture theatres. Your resilience, humour and humanity are what keep me moving forward, and I hope my words do you justice.

To Mike, Steve, Mark, Owen, Dan and Saul, thank you. It is your voices that tell this story with such power. I hope they will also be the conduit for meaningful change. To Craig and Martin, thank you for agreeing to an interview, and I apologise that I ran out of the space to do your words justice.

To Deneen and Oli, your work at Ferndown is a source of absolute inspiration. The work you do is tremendous, and I'm really pleased that anyone who reads this book will know about it.

To Susan, Andy, Ken and the Taking Boys Seriously (TBS) team, thank you. With the TBS principles, you have achieved something truly amazing. It's a real privilege to call you my friends.

To Jon R, my research partner in crime, thank you for helping me make sense of all this and keeping me entertained with stories of marathons in Disneyland.

To Ashley, one of the highlights of my working life has been watching the magic you weave for young people with your words and writing. You are the example that all educators should follow.

A huge thank you to Dan, Kate, Lousie, Eleanor, Aliki, Ashleigh, Vicky-Nenya, Jon and the rest of the team at Arts University Bournemouth for being my sanity for the entirety of the time it's taken me to write this book. Your support has been awesome, and you're the best colleagues a Blower could ask for.

Finally, a monumental thank you to Robyn, my beautiful, supportive, amazing partner. Thank you for being by my side for every wobble, crisis of confidence and minor breakdown. Your words of encouragement kept me going. You're the best, and I love you.

This book is dedicated to Charlie, my beautiful little boy. I love you with every fibre of my being.

1

Introduction: Standing on the shoulders of giants

Being a boy from a working-class town profoundly influenced my relationship with the world around me. It guided my interests, friendship groups and thoughts about the future. It set expectations for my behaviour and the way I treated people. These unwritten rules dictated how safe I felt to engage in education, and which emotions were permissible to display openly in front of others. During childhood, personal circumstances entwined with these expectations, leading to my experience of acute anxiety. I missed several years of formal education and was eventually excluded from school at age 13.

For the next decade, how I was expected to 'be a man' played an influential role in decisions to take drugs, engage in sexist behaviour and get into fights. Conflicting messages about what I had to do, and whom I had to be, led to bad decisions. A cycle of hurting myself and others. Chasing validation and acceptance from friends so that I could feel better about being me. In the world that I was a part of at the time, to be successfully masculine often meant inflicting harm. It could be physical or emotional, and it always came at a price. Shame. For each instance of hurt inflicted on to others, a small erosion of self-worth followed. In time, wounds deepened. Like many of my friends, I turned to self-medication. A drink, a smoke or a pill to temporarily numb the psychological and emotional sting of how it felt to be me. It's only now, after many years, that I have the tools to critically reflect on the journey. To develop and communicate an understanding of what may have been happening and why.

It took a lot of luck to find a different way to be me. To many, my adult self bears little resemblance to the young man who got excluded from school, which was the trigger for a significant shift in my educational fortunes. Two years after my expulsion, I passed enough GCSEs (the exams we sit in England at age 16) to get into sixth form. Fast forward five years and I was settling into student accommodation at a local university. Nearly a decade later, I was the proud owner of a 2.1 in Drama from the University of Wolverhampton. Several months after, I began working in a hostel for homeless young people. Since then, to the great amusement of my friends and family, I studied for a PhD and gained the title 'Dr Blower'. Nowadays, I spend most of my life as a professional coming up with ways to better support young people who, because of the inequalities they experience, are denied access to opportunities in education and work. As I sit at a laptop in my comfy office with a golden retriever occupying the floor next to me, I'd have laughed if you told me that this was how life was going to turn out when I was 13.

Well, I say what happened was luck, but it wasn't, not really. Due to a set of circumstances which were particularly unique to my situation and largely out of my control, I was slowly equipped with a set of experiences, skills and social connections. These were the tools I needed to identify a different path, an alternative understanding of who I was and who I could be. But perhaps more importantly, they provided me with the resources required to get there. The cognitive, social and cultural equipment necessary to plan for a future which involved continued engagement in education. A gradual repositioning in my perception of learning which meant that, instead of rejecting it as undesirable and effeminate, I began to embrace it.

For many of the young men I knew from school, this opportunity to find an alternative trajectory into manhood simply didn't exist. Growing up in a working-class town in the West Midlands, we lived our life in constant negotiation with unwritten rules and expectations about who we were supposed to be, conditions which were inscribed into the social fabric of our community. A lot of the boys I went to school with stayed on a trajectory toward a destination which our environment consistently reinforced as the most legitimate. It did so at school, at home, on the street and down at the pub. For some, it resulted in a good job in the trades, a nice house and a nice family. But for many, it did not.

For a lot of the young men from my hometown, life was characterised by circumstances which led to them contributing to some of the following statistics:

- Young men account are twice as likely to be excluded from school than young women.[1]
- Men account for 75 per cent of all deaths by suicide.[2]
- Men account for 70 per cent of the homeless population.[3]
- Men account for 96 per cent of the prison population.[4]
- Men account for 73 per cent of those in treatment for substance misuse.[5]

The anger, frustration and extreme sadness I feel when reading these statistics is my reason for writing this book. Alongside it being a subject in which I have developed a level of expertise, it is profoundly personal. I can attribute one or more names of young men I went to school with as a child to each of those statistics. Had I not been 'lucky' enough to experience a critical break in my own transition to manhood, I may not have escaped with only featuring in one of them. It is a snapshot of the challenges that young men, especially those who might not have the privilege of a 'comfortable' home life, face.

Yet in my view, for too long we have been getting the conversation surrounding what to do about it wildly wrong. If a young man is struggling with his mental health, we encourage him to open up to his friends more, yet at the same time we entrench societal beliefs around masculinity which condition young men to ridicule one another for displaying sadness. We blame young working-class men for having low aspirations but systematically strip away the mechanisms for higher educational hopes to be realised. We continually perpetuate a narrative which implies that the burden of responsibility for these 'failings' is theirs to carry alone. Whether it be school exclusion, death by suicide, homelessness or addiction, we present those outcomes as individual choices. Decisions which are detached, conscious and calculated.

The wrongness inherent in the type of conversation we have is demonstrated by the fact that for years, none of those statistics have changed. In political arenas, the absence of a constructive debate about what can be meaningfully done to address these masculine ills is almost deafening. Where activity has been undertaken in research to understand these issues, it has largely been carried out by feminist academics. If you are looking to explore how they may play out in the experiences of young men or women who are at a socio-economic disadvantage, or don't have the luxury of being White, then look no further than the likes of bell hooks,[6] Kimberlé Crenshaw,[7] Judith Butler,[8] Beverley Skeggs[9] and Niobe Way.[10] Each has contributed to a foundational understanding of how, in a society characterised by deep inequalities, some forms of masculinity serve to entrench and reproduce the most severe harms. However, what's notably absent from the list is the voice of men who share this view. Men who understand the consequences that the societal status quo holds for their brothers, sisters, children and grandchildren. Men who have navigated the risks to their education and future relationships that a mix of socio-economic inequality and rigid expectations about what it means to be a man pose. A movement of male educators, researchers and youth practitioners who want to change the rules of the game for young working-class men who might be encountering similar challenges. This book includes some of those voices, setting out a roadmap toward a more hopeful future.

But it's quite a task. Expectations surrounding what constitutes 'appropriate' masculine behaviour seep into nearly every aspect of our existence. In the arenas of media, politics, work, sport, health, leisure, the criminal justice system and the family, these gendered relationships will play out in subtly different, yet similar ways. A breadth of settings, contexts and relationships which constitute the multifaceted shape of our day to day. They are components of complex societal machinery which, in its current configuration, serves to reproduce and compound the inequalities people experience. The machine is ancient, but it is also fluid. It adapts and updates in a continual dialogue with the actions of those responsible for its operation and care. Given the scale of the challenge, it would take a lot more than this short book to explore the entirety of such a complex issue. It would also take someone with far more knowledge and experience on the issues than I can bring to bear.

With that in mind, the text sets out to bring the gifts that I do possess to the table. Through a combination of my own journey, academic research and the voices of other men who have encountered similar challenges along the way, the book provides a means by which we can begin to view the educational experience of young working-class men in a different light. It will not examine every piece of societal machinery at play, and I make no apologies for that. Applying what I have learned on my journey so far to areas outside of those in which I hold the relevant expertise and experience would not do anyone any good. In fact, I believe attempts to do just that are part of the reason why we find ourselves in this position in the first place. There is a lot this book doesn't cover, even in the field of education where most of the conversation is located. It doesn't, to any great extent, deal with young men's engagement with social media manfluencers like Andrew Tate[11] or the damage caused by early exposure to content such as pornography online. However, what it does do is provide readers with a means to start thinking differently about young men's relationships to these things.

As discussed, a lot of what I talk about is not necessarily news to academics who have made it their life's work to investigate and understand these issues. In fact, a couple of them are interviewed in this book. Rather, it aims to make that understanding accessible. Complex discussions and ideas will not be presented in seven syllable words and long paragraphs. Instead, these ideas will be explored with the humanity the individuals concerned deserve. They will be introduced through a series of stories, some of which will be my own to tell, some of which will be those of others. Working-class men, young and old, who have navigated the complexities of masculine expectations. For those who are older and have 'made it' to middle-class professions, it will explore how they have used these experiences to fuel a sense of purpose. To drive their own personal missions to create happier, more fulfilling futures for young men who might have lived experiences which hold similarities to their own. Through the stories of the younger men, we draw a deeper understanding of the physical, social and psychological risks associated with being a young working-class man, both inside and outside the school classroom.

Engaging with a mix of conversations, reflections and research, the book shines a light on some of the men who are standing on the shoulders of giants. Using their deep understanding of the harm caused by our societal structures to mitigate some of the injury it inflicts upon marginalised young men, and those around them, in education. In its latter stages, the book will turn its focus to the future. It will consider what we have learned and how we might move forward in a more equitable direction. With a specific focus on education, it offers new and exciting opportunities. The final chapters provide detail on the how, with examples from where this learning has already made an impact. A new, more equitable approach to engage with young working-class men in education. An introduction to a burgeoning movement which, if nurtured, could chart a path toward the world I would like for my little boy.

But before we get to all that, I'm going to tell you a little bit more about me.

2

Masculinity and mental health: the big red button

My battle with anxiety began at nine years of age. One morning, I remember being woken up by my dad coming into my room. He looked unsteady on his feet, began to sway and crashed into the built-in wardrobe opposite my bed. Scared and confused, I yelled for my mum.

The next thing I remember was walking past the ambulance parked right outside my house on my way to school. Later sitting in a small classroom only a stone's throw away, I desperately wanting to climb out of the window and run back home.

When the school day ended, Mum picked me up and took me straight to the hospital. On our way, she told me that dad had done something silly, but that he was OK. The following weeks were a blur of daily hospital visits. First to a regular one, then one that mum described as being for people whose 'brains weren't very well'. Wards, doctors, nurses and people in suits. Other patients who, as a little boy, were funny and scary in equal measure. Many years after the incident, I would learn that the events of that morning were down to a mix of prescription medication and alcohol which my dad had intentionally taken. Many years later still, I would learn that this was accompanied by my mum finding a note.

Back then, my dad was drinking heavily and regularly. At this point during my childhood, his poor mental health and his battle with addiction combined to make life volatile for everyone in his orbit. He was at his lowest and seemed determined to sink deeper. I never felt fearful of my dad; he's not a violent person. Not in the

7

slightest. But the intensity of his emotions, fuelled by the drinking, were like a tsunami. I constantly worried he would be swept away.

Some of my earliest memories include holding him while he cried and calming him when he yelled. Doing my best to patch and mend the tears in relationships threatening to rip our little family apart. While I had brothers and sisters, it was only me and my mum and dad in the house. My siblings were older, protected by the independence that came with the advancement of their years. Deliberately shielded from the reality of life at home through brief phone calls and the performance we put on for their occasional visits.

I would have struggled to articulate it to anyone when I was little, but I knew how I interacted with Dad was important. When I spoke to him, he would sometimes hear me in a way that he didn't hear Mum. He would listen, and sometimes he would calm down. He needed me; they needed me. I knew that something terrible might happen if I wasn't there. In my nine-year-old brain, this wasn't something I could intellectualise or articulate; it was a feeling of certainty that I carried in my core.

Sitting in that classroom after the ambulance had come for my dad was the first time I felt it. Heart pounding. Sweat. Adrenaline. Fear. Panic. *Anxiety.*

It started off small. Feeling homesick during an overnight stay at a friend's house and having to go home. Emotional outbursts when my parents asked someone else to keep an eye on me while they did something without giving me any prior warning. In the months that followed, it grew in frequency and intensity. After a particularly traumatic week away at a Scout camp where an attempt was made to 'cure it', the anxiety and its implications began to take over my life.

Back at school on the first day of year six. It struck again. This time, I did climb out of the window, and I ran. Every time things felt unfamiliar or unsafe, anxiety was there. My body screaming to get out, to escape, to just get home and everything will be alright. It became a pattern for the next three years. I didn't go to school. I couldn't. I missed formative years of my education, and I missed making friends. But back then that wasn't important, what was important was home. Home was where I was needed. Home was where I felt safe. Usually.

During that time, my bedroom became my fortress. My best friends were our dog, Meg, and the Harry Potter books. I would read them and re-read them, wishing I could magic away the feelings. When the fortress was breached by the outside world, panic set in. I was willing to do anything to avoid that fist-clenching feeling brewing in the pit of my stomach. The first warning of what was to follow. I remember a morning before school when I must have been about ten or eleven, sitting with my legs dangling outside my bedroom window and mustering the courage to jump out on to the concrete driveway below. If I broke my legs, I wouldn't have to go to school.

As time passed over the next two years, the anxiety eroded my sense of freedom. The fortress of my bedroom turned into a prison. A constant internal battle raged between a desire to do things that everybody else seemed able to and terror of the possible implications. Sitting there, oscillating between anger and fear. Incapacitating terror that the condition which 'must-not-be-named' would once again slither its way into my thoughts, feelings and actions. Day after day, sitting in a room with a Harry Potter,[1] wishing that someone could magic it away.

Reflecting on this period of my life in more recent times has led me to notice some similarities between my experiences and those I'm sure my dad must have encountered as a young man going to school in the late 1950s. Although I don't know much about his childhood, I know it was a greatly traumatic period. My grandad was in the military. So, as is the norm for young people from forces families, the first years of my dad's life were spent moving around army bases. He spent time in Germany and various other European countries. My grandfather was also an alcoholic and died when my dad was very young. I can only speculate, but I would assume my grandfather also fought his own intense battles with mental ill health, exacerbated no doubt by his reliance on the drink.

For my dad, the consequences of experiencing his father's death at such a young age were seismic. How he felt at the time is not something I've ever asked him about. I try to place myself in his shoes as a little boy, and I can't comprehend the injury that such an experience would inflict. Compounding his grief, shortly after his father's death, my dad was sent away to a military boarding school.

He describes his time there as the worst days of his life. Over the years, he's recounted small segments of his experience to me. The worst was bullying and torment at the hands of his schoolmates, something which was endured day and night in an unending cycle. Running away from the school and making it home, only to be sent straight back to the place he was escaping from.

My dad is dyslexic, autistic and incredibly intelligent and sensitive. Back in the 1950s, neither condition was understood or discussed in mainstream educational research,[2] let alone recognised within the state education system.[3] Alongside the bullying, his learning difficulties affected his education and how he processed the world around him. Due to his difficulties with literacy, teachers wrote him off as 'thick'. He puts the fact that he properly learned to read and write as a teenager down to a single teacher who took the time to work with him.

Once Dad had the tools to properly embark on his journey as a learner, he never stopped. He loves words and English, old buildings and historic battles, the psychology of human decision making and the workings of the social world which influence them. He trained as a teacher and worked with young people who had special educational needs in the 1980s. He worked in prisons with individuals in the criminal justice system and at colleges of further education. When he was well, he went for jobs which allowed him to support people who may have experienced similar challenges to his own. In the 1980s and early 1990s, he found his purpose, worked toward it and found it incredibly rewarding.

However, these early life experiences were akin to a fire. Sometimes a smoulder and sometimes an inferno. The growing intensity of the heat continued to cause psychological and emotional damage, burning my dad throughout his life. For many, many years, alcohol was my dad's medication. A way to take the edge off, to numb the pain and soothe the burn. In much the same way as it has been passed from my grandfather to my dad, the baton of intergenerational trauma fell into my hands.

It weighed heavily, the implications of their respective ailments cascading into my interactions socially and educationally. Over two years, the last of primary and the first of secondary, the time I spent at school was next to non-existent. If I did go, it was for parts of days, or not at all. When too much pressure was exerted by my parents or professionals, months of progress with my attendance could be undone in a second. It was paradoxical because inside, I desperately wanted to be there.

The more time I spent out of school not doing what everyone else did, the more I drifted toward the social margins. Less time in class, less time in the playground, fewer friends. When I was at school, I was confronted with a barrage of constant questions about why I was different. Why do you go home at breaktime? Why can't you last a full day at school? Why are you crying and shouting again? As a ten-year-old, I didn't have the equipment in my cognitive toolkit to answer these questions. I just got angrier and more upset.

It prompted unkindness from the other children that was perhaps borne out of a misplaced jealousy. There were loads of other kids who didn't like school in my class. They still had to be there, so why did I get to go home?

I missed out on important preparation for the year six SAT tests, but I took them. I even did OK considering. But graduation from primary school simply transported my difficulties to a significantly larger, more complex arena.

My secondary school was one of two in the town where I grew up, with the catchment area pretty much split down the middle. Both serviced a predominantly working-class local population and were often attended by multiple generations of young people from the same families. Two of my half-sisters on my mum's side, both over 15 years my senior, attended the school. One had even been taught science by the same teacher I ended up having in my first year. It should have been a place which was comfortable and familiar, like a special edition of Monopoly where it looks a bit different, but you still know all the rules. It wasn't.

On the first day, I really, really tried to be normal, but I failed.

By 3 pm, I was back at home, shouting, crying and planning everything I could think of to avoid being forced to return the next day. To my mind, this new school was a concrete monster, a place full of strange people, rooms and corridors intent on doing me harm. Stopping me being safe. Again, just like in primary school, I was absent for long periods. The school wanted me there more regularly, but after rewards didn't work and threats made matters worse, staff were stuck. I believe they genuinely wanted to help, but I was one of over a thousand students they had to think about. Whether it be money, time or expertise, they just weren't set up for dealing with someone like me and the difficulties I was navigating.

When I was in school, the status of outsider – which became embedded in primary school – was firmly cemented. Jeering and taunts in the corridors – 'there's the pussy who can't even last a day at school'. Being followed around by other students, whispering in my ear about my weakness, my worthlessness, calling me a woman. Once again, I was shoved firmly to the social margins. An outsider, a weird curiosity who was often observed in a state of extreme emotional distress. For some, it was funny. A few of the lads in my year made creating the conditions which led to those outbursts a bit of a personal challenge.

After many months, gradually, I got better at going in. Through a lot of hard work from my parents, teachers and eventually social workers, I was back in school full time by the Christmas of my second year. I was back, yes, but I was still an outsider. Still socially isolated. Still an easy target. Under such pressure, I quickly learned the things that, as a young man, were likely to draw undesirable attention. Putting my hand up in class and getting a question right. Not wearing my uniform in a scruffy enough way, acting like I cared about learning or the feelings of others. Not enthusiastically joining in with the bullies when the opportunity arose.

Then there were the things that reaped rewards, an uplift in status among classmates and protection from becoming the target. Being rude to teachers, getting into fights, smoking and drinking. Being loud, being aggressive, acting like you didn't care about anything. Constantly vying to be tougher, stronger, ruder, louder. If you were good at sport or had a hard brother, you received an automatic boost in the hierarchy of masculine status at the school, but I wasn't a lad who had access to any of these assets. I had to rely on other means.

I quickly learned to stop doing the things that would paint me as a target, a juicy victim for breaktime and the walk home.

I mobilised the tools at my disposal to mitigate the risk of physical and emotional harm. To accomplish a position in the social hierarchy which meant I wasn't the first and most easy target. Now that I was there all the time, I realised that secondary school wasn't about learning, it was about survival.

Of course, at the time my thinking was nowhere near as nuanced as this reflection on my experience. I didn't realise that what I was doing was deliberately altering my identity as a young man at school. Changing my interests and behaviours to align with a way of being a teenage boy which would provide status. Instead, it was based on immediate gratification. The feeling of acceptance after an appreciative laugh in the classroom following something rude or stupid that I'd said to a teacher. An arm around the shoulder after knocking a 'weaker' kid's schoolbooks out of their hands in the corridor. Selling cigarettes to my classmates. Giving them out for free to the older kids when they asked. Being someone of value. It all sparked a dopamine hit that came with feeling accepted, feeling like I belonged. I'd start fights with other young men who were tougher or more popular than myself. I lost most, but the fact that I was seen getting into them did me a favour. Less of an easy target.

I started to get invited to local parks in the evening with older lads who were more popular. Smoking weed, drinking, breaking into places, setting fires and stealing things. Whether it be stealing money to get drunk and waking up in Good Hope Hospital, going joy riding in a car that a mate had managed to pick up for 50 quid from a scrap yard or waiting around the corner of someone's home to 'jump them' when they left, I caused damage. Damage to people, damage to property and damage to myself.

The overarching emotion I now feel about my experiences during this period is one of shame. Shame for the things I did, and shame for the hurt I caused. Regret for not having the strength to do what was right, rather than what was easy. For standing by rather than speaking up.

The memory which brings this about most acutely is the day I got excluded from school. In hindsight, it was the natural conclusion of the path I had purposely put myself on. At the age of 13, I got caught smoking a joint at lunchtime. Idiotically, I had decided to do this on one of the school field's most conspicuous places. A young history teacher spotted me and a 'mate' about to light up behind a mobile classroom at lunchtime. At first, he thought it was a roll-up cigarette and confiscated it, but he later found out that its contents were a little more ... problematic. Whether it was the shape, the smell or his previous 'experience', I'm not sure how he found out, but he did.

An hour later, a staff member came into my French lesson to take me to the Headteacher's Office. I remember the stony silence. Everyone around me knew where I was going and why. I rose to my feet and slowly walked to the door, feeling nervous, numb and incredibly stupid.

I wasn't the first student at the school to smoke weed at lunchtime, but the Deputy Head informed me I was the first who was stupid enough to get caught. My parents were called, meetings were had, and I was never allowed to return. After years of helping me navigate my acute anxiety, my mum going part time with her work so she could support me and my dad, after countless meetings with educators, mental health professionals and social workers, all to get me back into school, I had rewarded them with being expelled.

It's only many years later after a lot of reflection, experience working in education and my research behind me that I can start to piece together the complexity of what was happening to me. For a long time afterward, I was stuck in a rut, one which extended the legacy of those experiences well into adulthood. They became an arsenal of attitudes, behaviours and actions linked inextricably to who I was. They informed conversations with friends and the things I got up to at the weekend. They influenced my approach to relationships and my treatment of others. An amalgamation of ways to be me which eroded wellbeing and my ability to maintain healthy relationships. During this time, I treated a lot of people, myself included, horribly.

To start with, it all happened subconsciously. A way of being so ingrained into my identity as a young man that it was automatic. Not just for me, but for my friends too. We'd grown up in the same town and gone to the same school. A shared experience which created unsaid expectations for social interactions and group dynamics. Codes of behaviour which, when adhered to, still provided that addictive rush of instant gratification linked to feeling as though you belong. But they had consequences. Shame which seared my psyche every time I gave in to behaviour which was misogynistic and harmful. A big red button which, when pressed, sent a hit of dopamine from acceptance with no thought to the blast radius created. Thoughts about the fallout did come, but later. A moral self-audit generating a cascade of guilt and shame; the rush of self-loathing which hit whenever I closed my eyes to go to sleep.

Even now, after years of social and geographic distance from many of those friends, sitting at a desk in my office after having achieved 'the dream' of a decent salary and a cushy middle-class job, that big red button remains. One that I know I shouldn't touch but have a near insatiable urge to press. All those dispositions, the ways of acting and being which are so tightly bound to physical and psychological self-injury are there, still alluring. The automatic association I have with pressing the button, even though I'm incredibly aware of it, still whispers a promise of improved social status, being rewarded, a big hit of gratification and acceptance. Of course, I now know that very few of those things will be the objective outcome of giving it a good old whack, but it's the result of years of inculcation, and the foundations were laid at school.

What happens at school, that space we go to day in, day out from the age of four until the age of 16 is important. The way we're taught, what we're asked to learn, our relationship with educators and our relationship with peers mould us. They help to form our interests, our relationships and our understanding of the wider world. The reflections in this chapter are just a small part of the contribution it played in shaping my life. It makes sense that, if there are issues linked to young men and masculinity, these formative years may be a useful place to look in conversations to address the problematic elements.

Over the years, I've encountered several organisations that deliver interventions targeted at young working-class men in education. Boys whose experiences may resonate in some way, shape or form with those described in this chapter. It is rare, however, that those encounters have left me feeling enthused and hopeful. All too often, those who are leading the activity share very little in common with the young men. Not in terms of gender – during my time in education, I've worked with some fantastic practitioners, men and women, who have built amazing relationships with young men and made a positive impact on their lives. No, when I talk of things in common, I refer to an understanding of what their life might be like. A deep empathy toward some of the challenges that come with growing up without the socio-economic safety nets many take for granted. An appreciation of their lives and experiences as worthwhile, and a shared understanding of their uniqueness and complexity.

In many examples, I have seen a stark absence of such understanding. Instead, the interventions are designed through assumptions of what these young men 'need' based on stereotypes and ideological positions. It bleeds into programme design. Projects which are based on the premise that young working-class men have a deeply ingrained deficiency which needs to be corrected. Young working-class men, many of whom have already experienced acute marginalisation, are positioned as problematic through their very existence. Activities and 'interventions' are designed on the premise that they are perpetrators of misogyny and gender-based violence in waiting, even if they are not aware of it yet. Often, they are conducted with no thought to the implications for the young men themselves. The fact that, because of the limitations imposed by our societal structure, these same young people are more likely to die by suicide, more likely to experience homelessness, more likely to battle with substance misuse and more likely to enter the criminal justice system.

Within these 'interventions', there is little recognition that those same societal structures and systems inflict great harm on the young men in the classroom too. Trauma which is often exacerbated by the material inequality they face. Instead of initiatives designed to empower, support and educate young men about such issues, schemes of work are established which blame them. Well-meaning adults heap the burden of responsibility for such societal ills squarely on their shoulders. Lessons which ooze a with a silent implication, placing the blame for the pernicious products of gender-based inequality at the feet of the boys and young men sitting in front of them. Within such a worldview, responsibility for fixing it is theirs and theirs alone.

In *The Will to Change: Men, Masculinity and Love*,[4] bell hooks offers a different and important perspective. Widely regarded as one of the greatest thinkers and activists on issues relating to race and gender inequality in our time, hooks' writing encapsulates the very essence of the problem with approaches made on such an assumptive premise. She argues that it is not that such activities fail to recognise the evils of patriarchal societal systems and structures – they often do so vociferously. Rather it is that, through their work, there is an absence of understanding, care and compassion for the young men who may be the recipients. It's not intentional. The activity largely comes from a good place. It's grown from a desire to do the right thing in tackling significant societal harms. However, the omission of any value afforded to the lives and experiences of the young men is deafening. Rather than being a conduit to new ways of thinking and feeling for the young men involved, they feel attacked. Instead of, as hooks describes, their inner lives being valued, the approach dismisses them as inconsequential and unimportant. Sadly, rather than cultivating connection and shared understanding, it alienates, doing more harm than good.

Mike

For several years during and immediately after my PhD, which finished in 2020, I had resigned myself to this approach being 'just how it was'. I tried on numerous occasions, while working for several different organisations in the preceding five years, to instigate projects based on a more strengths-based approach. A way of working which focused on empowering young men to engage educationally, recognising the importance of their lives and experiences. Sessions and activities which provided the equipment for boys and young men to decide what a happy, healthy future looked like. Working alongside them, I wanted to create the conditions to cultivate their aspirations into expectations, facilitating an exploration of their imagined opportunities, lifestyle and relationships. Time and time again, I failed to get them off the ground.

My efforts failed for the very reason described earlier. Back then, there was little understanding of how young working-class men's educational disengagement was entangled within wider issues surrounding misogyny and gender-based inequality. A lack of recognition that they were two pieces of the same puzzle. No matter how hard I tried, I couldn't seem to break through with a message which didn't begin with framing the young men as 'the problem'. Luckily, it was around that time that someone else was beginning to.

Taking a break from the screen on my laptop one day back in 2021 to spend some time with my other smaller, mobile phone screen, I was scrolling through Twitter (now X) and came across an organisation called Progressive Masculinity.[5] They were exciting. Led by a guy called Mike Nicholson, an ex-teacher, Progressive Masculinity offered a social and emotional learning programme for young men which claimed to place young men's interpretation of masculinity at the centre of their work.

So, naturally, I reached out. After a brief Twitter exchange, I met Mike on a Teams call for the first time in late 2021. We immediately realised that we had an awful lot in common both personally and professionally. Hailing from Bury, an ex-industrial town near to Manchester, Mike's life growing up in a working-class family has been instrumental in shaping his view of the world. From getting into slanging matches with local kids who attended the local grammar school through holes in fences which separated their school playing fields, to navigating university life as one of a minority of students from a working-class background who attended a Russell Group university (an 'elite' self-selected association of public research universities in the UK), Mike's own negotiation of social mobility played a formative role in the development of his professional identity. Much like with my own journey, his reflections on his experiences also instilled within him a critical perspective on the elements of his own transition to manhood which he has struggled to navigate:

> I hit a critical point where I thought you can't keep doing this now. The self-loathing has got to a point where I need to change. I need to start making some better decisions. You know, I shouldn't be shouting things like that at that girl or I shouldn't be pretending that I'm better than a lad who is a lot less athletic than I am, because I'm not. There's nothing special about

being good at football. It was a slow accumulation of experiences that made me realise I need to make better decisions.

While of course there were differences, our respective journeys through education and life afterward had led us to a similar place. His experiences resulted in the formulation of a set of core principles on which he built his personal and professional identity. Recognising that the education system placed restrictions on what he could achieve as a teacher, he decided to branch out and in the process created an entirely new business. He committed his energy into supporting some of society's most marginalised young men in education. While I was working in universities, he was working in school classrooms. Not as a teacher, but as something different. An alternative professional identity which embodied a commitment to flattening hierarchies, building trust and fostering meaningful connection.

Following wave after wave of positive feedback about his sessions from educators, Mike is now a regular speaker at some of the UK's most prestigious teacher conferences. His work is great, and schools love it. Last year, I had the opportunity to sit in on a series of Progressive Masculinity's workshops at a school a few miles down the road from my home in Bournemouth.

Working with a group of 12 young working-class men aged 13 and 14, the two-day workshop and its highly interactive content afforded the opportunity for the participants to discuss their perceptions of what it meant to be a man. It engaged with societal perceptions of masculinity and how they were internalised by the young men involved. The differences between what they thought and felt, and the pressures they felt to act in certain ways which made them feel uncomfortable. It covered friendships, social media and dealing with difficult emotions. Although the content was very good, it wasn't what left a lasting impression. It was the energy in the room. While at the beginning the young men were a little stand offish and covering nerves with laughter and bravado, very quickly the room became a place of safety and honesty. There was no risk of judgement for expressing thoughts and opinions; instead, they were encouraged to engage in critical conversation about their perceptions and why they held them.

They shared things, discussed things and built a connection with the facilitator and one another. For Mike and the team, creating these conditions is central to their work.

Having worked as a teacher for 18 years before embarking on his new vocation, Mike combines his lived and professional experiences, occupying a space somewhere between teacher and youth worker. In doing so, he appears to have found a way to gain a level of autonomy. A refreshing flexibility which unlocks the ability to have deeper, more constructive conversations with young men about the role of masculinity inside and outside the classroom. While challenging, the sessions centralise the value of the young men's thoughts, feelings and experiences as pivotal to exploration of the topics they engage with.

Initially developed in collaboration with three female colleagues, the programme grew out of a module Mike developed for students surrounding attitudes to women while working as a teacher:

> During that time, I spent a lot of time mentoring, particularly young boys, who other people found difficult and challenging, and it was often in an unofficial capacity at breaktime, dinnertime, before school, after school. There are certain people in the school that boys like that feel safe talking to. I'm quite glad that I was one of those. When I'm speaking to all these different boys who encounter all these different issues, the underlying thread that connected them all was this performance of masculinity that they were all living. I knew there was so much there that they weren't showing. They were sabotaging their relationships and their academics, all to live by an image that had been socially and culturally put together. An image which influenced and conditioned them to think they had to behave in certain ways to be a man. So, I went to the headteacher while I was still working. I said I've got this idea, and I put a programme together.

While Mike designed the module to directly engage with attitudes to women, he foregrounded the importance of what it meant for the young men involved, their *inner lives*. Mike explored how masculinity impacted on their future educational opportunities, and what it meant for their ability to maintain healthy relationships with people they loved. It wasn't about framing them and their behaviour as dangerous, it wasn't about discovering what they might want to do when they left school. Instead, the programme focused on who they wanted to be as a man and why.

Located near Manchester, Progressive Masculinity works alongside schools to develop policies, strategies and schemes aligned with their mission: promoting a more open-minded understanding of what it means to be 'a man'. In a world which can feel very isolating and confusing to young men, especially as they begin to negotiate their position within it, opening up this space is important. While there are several charities working in education to tackle misogyny in the classroom, what sets Progressive Masculinity apart is their strengths-based approach. Rather than taking a position which starts with blame, Mike embarks on an exploration alongside the young men, facilitating conversations which allow them to critically engage with thoughts and feelings about their lives, experiences and the role masculinity plays in how they engage with the world.

Mike's own experience of growing up in a working-class community has given him the ability to empathise with the young men and is a central pillar of his professional identity. Combining this with the pedagogic tools at his disposal, Mike emphasises the notion of empowerment within his work. Covering a range of areas including mental health and confidence, self-regulation, bullying, motivation and oracy, the programme is a guided exploration. A journey which values and prioritises the agency of the young men at every juncture.

Mike's decision to step out of teaching into the freer, but somewhat riskier, world of self-employment came from a desire to expand the breadth and depth of those educational relationships:

> As an English teacher, you wouldn't even get to choose the book anymore that you taught for that loss of autonomy. For the teachers, you know, teaching is a very human job. There should be no one way to do it. And I know a lot of teachers feel frustrated. They're cast between the devil and the deep blue sea. They

either do what they think is right for the pupil and stray from what you'd refer to as classic pedagogy, or they stick to what they're told to do, but they lose, you know, the relationships in the classroom.

Mike felt that to have the impact he desired on the young people he taught, he needed to have more freedom; a way to build more meaningful and authentic connections with the students. With what he described as 'one step' approaches to behaviour management and extremely prescriptive curriculums, Mike felt that rather than empowering young people to become active participants in their educational journey, school policies sometimes presented a barrier.

As Mike explained what he wanted to do as a teacher, but due to the constraints of the job, couldn't, I wondered how common the frustrations he voiced must be. Teachers across the country desperately wanting to do more, to build relationships which had greater depth and reciprocity but who were hamstrung in their ability to do so. For me, as a young man who just about survived in school prior to my expulsion, I was desperate for that type of relationship. I can't help wondering how different life in education would have looked if there was anyone there I felt safe to truly speak to. Someone to open up to about home, school, friends and the acute pressure I felt to fit in. To be included in a group while knowing that I couldn't afford to be the odd one out. For Mike, fostering this type of relationship is one of the things he values most in his work:

> What I value is that primacy of relationship. The first couple of sessions are extremely practical in nature. You know, we're up from our chairs. We're doing activities with a little bit of chatting after each, to break down what the key messages were. As the programme develops, it becomes less practical and more talk based because that's what generally we're not very good at as men, particularly with other men, is talking about real life issues.

The relationship he gradually builds with the young men, and the relationship they establish with one another, is paramount within his work. Rather than a hierarchy in which he is an 'expert' bestowing knowledge on the young men, their voices are valued and valuable. The thoughts, experiences and feelings of the young people in the room are assets within the learning journey. Through a gradual transition from practical activities to discussion-based activity within the programme, he slowly equips the young men with the tools required for critical engagement with masculinity's role within their own lives. A far cry from initiatives based on the premise that the young men are inherently deficient, his work focuses on empowerment. Providing a safe space and a vocabulary which enables them to speak about real life issues with other young men:

> One of the things that come across loud and clear is that they feel unseen and unheard. You know, they feel if they try to speak about a topic that isn't part of the lesson plan or goes against, you know, academic thinking at the time or whatever, that they're shut down. And that leads to extreme frustration for them. I say, like, don't worry about being too politically correct from the very start. Don't worry about your language too much. Just be real.
>
> A lot of the feedback on the evaluations you've probably seen on social media, they say things like 'No one has ever spoken to me like that before', or 'I didn't think we could speak like that before.' 'Men have never told me that I was OK to speak like that before', and that's obviously what the education system at the moment isn't providing them, it isn't providing them with a way for their strengths to be recognised or a way for their voice to be heard.

While interviewing Mike, I was struck by how ludicrous the situation surrounding engaging with young working-class men appeared. Here I was, sitting at my desk in 2023, with over half a decade of entrenched disparities in educational outcomes for working-class boys behind us, and what Mike was saying appeared to be that much of it could be addressed by listening. Providing a safe space in education for the young men to be heard. To be able to speak honestly about their thoughts and feelings without fear of judgement and reprisal. Of course, while it sounds deceptively simple, meaningfully engaging with a group of young men who have experienced marginalisation in education and wider society requires great skill and sensitivity. For Mike, his ability to generate such a set of conditions came as much from his lived experience as his training as an educator:

> Coming from the working-class background myself, I was never the kind of teacher or person that kind of pontificated about masculinity from a place of perfection. I was always very open, honest about my feelings and how I fell into a lot of the same pitfalls and traps of masculinity as a young man. How they brought me nothing but pain and suffering, and also the people around me. So I think being relatable to some of the young men with my honesty was a big thing for them. That kind of liberated them and made them feel safe, you know, with the same kind of issues.
>
> Modelling some of the things that I've done wrong. Not coming across the perfect man. Showing them examples of men who maybe are strong but compassionate, successful but also selfless. You don't need to be cruel. Being a man isn't about being cruel and aggressive all the time. Giving them these examples. Yeah. I think that's kind of why it took me four years to get all these different elements into a programme in the right order with the right structure to have that kind of impact.

In his own life, Mike hit a critical juncture, a realisation that his relationship with his own masculine identity needed to change. The feeling of self-loathing he described struck a chord. The way that, similar to myself, the desire to fit into a set of masculine behaviours which were deemed to hold most social currency had inflicted psychological and emotional injury. Whether it be bullying friends in the name of 'banter' or acts of misogyny, a gradual awareness of the psychological and emotional implications of the behaviour grew. Mike describes how it wasn't just the people around him who were damaged by these actions; it ate away at his esteem and sense of self – 'it wasn't a lightbulb moment, it was a slow accumulation of shame'. A growing awareness of the strong connection between his behaviour and his own wellbeing led him to make significant changes in his own life. He reflected that even now, after dedicating his career to supporting young men who experience these challenges, there are still aspects of his masculine identity which he struggles to reconcile with the father and husband he wishes to be.

What inspires me about Mike's life and his work is how he's taken hold of such experiences, flipping them on their head and using them to empower the young men he works with. Talking about some of the mistakes he's made, alongside providing examples of men who express their masculine identities in different ways, creates fertile ground in the classroom. Conditions which provide rich opportunities not just for learning but for the development of trust, rapport and connection. This openness and vulnerability mean that when he informs a group of young men who have been excluded from mainstream education that 'I care about who you want to be, not what you want to be', they tend to believe him:

> I mean, you know, pack mentality is strong for a reason because it's safe in the pack, isn't it? You're not isolated, you're not the target. I'm sure there's, you know, I'm sure there's some evolutionary survival benefit to being part of the pack. But the big push that I have is that there's nothing wrong with that. You know, social is what we need. We need strong connections. However, if you're part of a pack or a group that is going against what you know, your conscience is telling you is right, then you're gonna get risk either way. You're either choosing the personal risk of isolation and marginalisation because you were strong enough to stand up to it. Or you're pushing a risk of maybe getting into trouble with the law or losing that sense of self and identity, you know, by staying as part of that group.

Something which he is also acutely aware of is the risk he's asking them to take through their engagement with him in the programme. Within work which follows individualised, deficit-driven narratives, there is often little attention paid to the risk associated with a change in behaviour for the young men. The consequences of saying or doing something which you know may well lead to personal risk of isolation and marginalisation. Of a constant negotiation between what's right and what keeps you safe. Within his work, Mike leverages group dynamics to shift the mentality of 'the pack'. He builds coalitions with young men based on an agreed set of principles surrounding what a happy, healthy future might look like for them and guides reflection on what might need to happen, what might need to change, in order for them to get there.

On Mike's website, there is a quote by a year 11 student which reads 'These sessions made me feel like I don't have to pretend to be someone else. Someone I don't actually like being anyway.' For me, it encapsulates the power of Mike's work. Through valuing the primacy of the relationship and the inner lives of the young men above all, Mike creates subcultures where they can be uniquely themselves.

While in our interview it was clear that our experiences of growing up were very different, during the conversation with Mike I felt a connectedness to our journeys. A feeling that while we had both come a long way, pressure to perform in a certain way as a man was an ever-present companion. That red button, one which didn't just disappear because you were now in a position to read the big sign saying 'do not push'. And therein lies the issue. The work Mike conducts through Progressive Masculinity might shine a beacon of light, one which may guide others toward more equitable engagement with working-class boys and young men in education. However, he is also just one man. A wonderful anomaly within the vast network of educational and societal structures and systems which work in a very different way from that which he describes.

3

Social mobility: navigating
the aspiration trap

As a little boy, working for a university wasn't exactly high up on my list of desired career destinations. In fact, I didn't even know that the job I do existed.

Day to day, my role involves leading a small team to design and deliver creative projects with young people from backgrounds which are underrepresented in higher education. The work aims to provide opportunities to engage with creative subjects like animation, film or model making. For young people from more middle-class backgrounds, chances to engage in this type of learning are regular and numerous. For the young people we work with, they most certainly are not. With the decimation of creative subject provision in English state schools since 2010,[1] the sparsity of opportunity to study creative subjects at GCSE level has, unsurprisingly, been experienced most significantly by young people who are already likely to feel the tight squeeze of socio-economic inequality.[2]

In our work, we do our level best to swim against the tide. Attempting, despite the increasingly stark disparities in opportunity with secondary school curriculums, to cultivate the conditions whereby studying a creative subject at university could be framed as an expectation by the individuals we work with. Not as a fuzzy dream or ambition, but something they perceive as achievable and probable if it's something they'd like to pursue. To provide an illustrative example of its potential, we'll speak specifically to the impact of this work on a group of young men who were excluded from mainstream education later in the book.

But for now, the important thing is that when I finished my degree in drama back in 2010, I didn't know the job existed. Getting into it was pretty much an accident. After a brief spell in an elected role for my university's students' union, I got a job as a support worker in a hostel for homeless young people aged 16–25 in Birmingham. Although the pay and conditions were awful, those two years working at the hostel were some of the most important of my working life. Commencing my employment at the dawn of austerity under the Coalition government, I witnessed the consequences of political choices for working-class communities play out in front of my eyes. While I had my fair share of challenges growing up, they paled in comparison to those faced by some of the young adults I supported.

The job was difficult, but it was also really rewarding. During my time at the hostel, I worked with some fantastic colleagues. People I still look back to as a source of motivation and inspiration. But it was hard. Hard physically and hard emotionally. With very little prior training, I was suddenly the first line of triage for the acute challenges relating to poverty, addiction, violence and mental ill health that the young people in the hostel faced. As a young man who was still younger than many of the residents I supported, I quickly discovered the limitations of my drama degree in preparing me to handle the situations I encountered.

I like to think I'm fairly resilient, but the work took its toll. It was mentally and emotionally draining and, at times, dangerous. The pay was low. At the time I was employed, a support worker's salary was around £15,000 a year. Now, 12 years later, it sits at just under £20,000, and there are far, far fewer of them around.

After a particularly difficult shift, I got home, turned on the computer and began to look for a new job. I found an advert for a role at a local university working with schools and colleges. It paid about £8,000 per year more than I was on at the hostel and looked pretty easy, so I went for it. My experience studying at university, doing some volunteering with the students' union and more recent work at the hostel combined to tick most of the boxes in the job description. I gave a passable interview and got a foot in the door as the second-choice candidate.

Three months later, I began as an assistant in my first university outreach team. Basically, my job was to tour various careers fairs in schools and colleges, do some talks and host visits to the university for school groups. It felt like I'd hit the jackpot. The work was easy, the pay was good and everyone around me was convinced we were doing important work to tackle inequality. Raising the aspirations of young people so they would begin to align their hopes toward study in higher education.

However, something didn't sit right. In my first few weeks, I was introduced to a dataset which universities used to measure the proportion of people from certain geographic areas who go to university. Naturally, the first thing I did was type in my home postcode. The number 18 flashed up – 18 per cent of young people who lived in my hometown postcode went to university. Then I typed in the postcode of the school I moved to following my expulsion – 64 per cent.

Statistically, people from my hometown, my friends, were over three times less likely to access higher education because of where they lived. If they grew up 6 miles down the road, their probability of going to university at age 18 more than tripled. I've got friends from home with more talent in their little fingers than I've got in my entire being. Friends who had worked for years in jobs they were unhappy in, only to risk everything they had by going back to college, getting their GCSEs and going to university as mature students years later.

I'd sat next to them in the local library, men in their late 20s and early 30s, consoling them as they fought the creeping tendrils of stress, anxiety and inadequacy that being a mature student had wrapped around them. Failing an assignment didn't just mean a bad grade; it risked stability, financial security, housing, relationships. *Everything*.

But they didn't buckle under this pressure, quite the opposite. They achieved grades that I could only ever dream of attaining. Now they work helping people, counsellors and nurses working with some of the most vulnerable groups in society. They are amazing. But through no fault of their own, they were denied the opportunity to do those things, learn those things, *be* those things at a time when the risks were less pronounced. At a time when they weren't risking a roof over their head, or their family's financial security. An opportunity withheld because they had the audacity to be born in the wrong postcode area.

Reading the data, reflecting on the experiences of my friends and the young people at the hostel, I became angry. Rather than my work just being a cushy job for a university, it became about something different. Staff at the university had access to money and resources that I could only ever have dreamed of working with at the hostel. Being there presented an opportunity, a way to make change and do better by people like my friends.

I began to read, to examine how we did things. To question how they worked and why. There was a lot of talk of 'raising aspirations', of lifting young people's hopes and ambitions for the future. But I couldn't see, given the experiences in education and work that I had, how asking them to set their sights higher would be enough. How, given the challenges faced by these young people, encouraging them to dream of a future which involved higher education could mitigate against the social and educational barriers they encountered.

If I'm honest, it didn't even really feel like we were working with the right students. Most of the young people I spoke to in schools already appeared to be on an educational journey which already included university in the future. We got called into sixth forms, pedalling our wares in front of students who had comfortably passed their GCSEs but perhaps didn't know much about the university application process. We wouldn't go into colleges and work with the thousands of students who had failed in their maths and english exams and were currently retaking them, even though we knew that most of them were young people from working-class backgrounds.

I rarely spoke with the other students. The ones teachers wouldn't select for visits because they weren't expected to get the grades, or the ones actively excluded from assembly talks and classroom presentations on the basis that they were 'troublemakers'. It resulted in a situation where, much of the time, it felt like I was actively discouraged from working with the young people I believed would benefit most from support and opportunities.

I found myself working within a model which felt fundamentally flawed. This wasn't just happening at my university but right across the country. I'd sit in presentation after presentation delivered by colleagues at practitioner conferences which told the same story in different ways. Thousands of hours of activity by universities with schools and colleges, designed to raise the aspirations of young people toward higher education. However, for most students these projects engaged with, it was a destination which already seemed to be the likely outcome.

I couldn't articulate how or why at the time, but I couldn't shake the feeling that we were pointing ourselves in the wrong direction. That we weren't working with the right young people in the right way. I felt frustrated at how little I really knew about how educational inequality worked, and why no one really seemed to mind that we rarely worked with those who were most actively excluded from educational opportunity. Thinking back to the experiences of my friends, I couldn't help but reflect on what the university outreach work would have achieved for them at school. Young men who had complex home lives and weren't 'gifted and talented'. Boys who were removed from lessons and got into trouble as a way to protect themselves, to guard against the risk of harm. The conclusion I reached was that it would have achieved very little.

So, in 2016 I became a student again. This time doing a PhD with a special interest in inequality and access to higher education for working-class boys in the West Midlands. I wanted to understand the real reason why so few of them passed their exams, and why such a small proportion progressed to university.[3] I was committed to deepening my understanding of inequality, to use the knowledge to do better by the young men we purported to serve. As an experience, it was invaluable.

The most useful part of my PhD wasn't conducting research or becoming a 'Dr'; it was access to the treasure trove of knowledge about experiences of inequality which I felt a deep connection to. Articles and books full of ways I could begin to articulate the things I could feel but didn't understand enough to explain to anyone else. I learned why we needed to move away from well-trodden, potentially harmful stereotypes and tropes about working-class young men being 'aspirationally deficient'. How universities which worked to a deficit model often did more harm than good, and why approaches which focused on young people's strengths were important. I began to understand the instrumental importance of work which held valuing the richness and diversity of young men's communities, geographies, cultures and histories at its very heart. Using them as vehicles to promote social justice and drive meaningful change. To build narratives which actively contested the idea that inequality is an individual 'choice' and instead focus on how inequality is felt and what we can do to address it. To remove the burden of responsibility for experiences of inequality from the shoulders of young people and their families and work to address the root causes. The machinery built into the fabric of society which entrenches and reproduces these inequalities across generations.

I learned that if we wanted to do things differently, we had our work cut out.

So, I began exploring, finding accessible ways to get this knowledge that people needed to hear into the head of people who needed to hear it. Academics are very good at producing knowledge but not necessarily at using it effectively once it's created. I wanted people like me to be able to use it. Individuals who didn't spend all of their time reading, writing and talking about what they'd read and written. It needed to get into the brains of practitioners, people who taught, educated and supported. Professionals who may have had that same feeling which they couldn't quite put their finger on. A hunch that something wasn't right, but they couldn't quite describe how.

Later chapters will provide some specific examples of how powerful such an approach can be when mobilised in practice. But first, it is important to understand how we reached such a position in the first place. An unconscious, taken-for-granted assumption that the 'problem' with working-class young people, especially boys, was a lack of aspiration. A narrative which, since the time of Blair's Government has become a national obsession for policy makers and educators alike.

High aspirations: the silver bullet to inequality?

For nearly as long as I've been alive, aspiration has been viewed by policy makers as a silver bullet in tackling inequality and promoting social mobility within the UK. It has been lauded to the nation as an instrument by which working-class people who experience material inequality can become middle class. A way to level the playing field, creating greater equality of opportunity so that those from humble beginnings can 'reach the top'. First emerging in the late 1990s, it was a totemic feature of New Labour policy. It marked the beginning of a narrative which, in the following decades, would leave a significant imprint on the way the nation understood educational inequality and what should be done about it.

Following Labour's landslide election victory in 1997, Tony Blair used his victory speech to call for a nation which could 'meet the challenges of an entirely new century and new age'.[4] Blair's vision of an educated, aspirational workforce was a key component of the new world he was introducing. In the following years, the notion of aspiration was increasingly adopted as a tool by which, it was believed, greater social mobility could be achieved. It became a regular feature of national conversations about education, work and welfare eventually taking residence as a key ideological feature of government policy.

Following Labour's defeat at the general election in 2010, the torch of aspiration was passed on to the newly elected Coalition government. In 2011, the White Paper 'Opening doors, breaking barriers: a strategy for social mobility' was published, which claimed that 'every child in our country deserves a world-class education. The education system should challenge low aspirations and expectations, dispelling the myth that those from poorer backgrounds cannot aim for top universities and professional careers.'[5]

In 2012, at the Conservative Party Conference, Prime Minister David Cameron positioned himself as the leader of an 'aspiration nation'.[6] For both the Coalition and the New Labour government before them, the reason for restricted social mobility was the level of ambition held by those who were most 'disadvantaged' in society. It was argued that this 'lack of drive' among those who experienced material inequality played a key role in restricting their ability to change their circumstances. This narrative implied that young people from 'non-privileged' backgrounds were unlikely to have high aspirations about what they wanted to achieve in later life. Moreover, it suggested that a change in their economic circumstance was something for which they held individual responsibility and therefore the power to change.

The political finger pointed directly toward this individual lack of ambition to 'reach the top' as a central concern in addressing societal inequality and promoting social mobility within working-class communities. The persistent rhetoric and resultant political focus laid down the foundation for an idea which has since become a taken-for-granted assumption among large swathes of educators and members of the public. The notion that young men from working-class backgrounds have a 'poverty of aspiration'.

Since the Brexit referendum in 2016, the COVID-19 pandemic in 2020 and most recently the cost-of-living crisis and global tensions surrounding the wars in Ukraine and Palestine, the political and media conversation around aspiration and social mobility has been less prominent. However, during its decades-long stint at the top of the political pops, it's had an undeniable impact on the approach taken by educators in attempts to grapple with the impact of inequality in education.

In 2016, the Higher Education Policy Institute produced a report which cited anecdotal evidence from Leicestershire City Council claiming that 'white working-class culture is characterised by low aspirations and negative attitudes to education in a way not seen with other ethnic groups'.[7] In 2018, Amanda Spielman, the chief of the Office for Standards in Education, Children's Services and Skills, gave a conference speech in which she claimed that poor White communities lack *aspiration and drive*.[8] While, as will be discussed later, these notions are heavily contested, they have nonetheless come to be seen as 'common sense'. The idea that young men from working-class backgrounds, especially if they are from deindustrialised communities in the North of England like Sheffield, Newcastle or Morcombe, are characterised by deficiencies in hope or ambition has become synonymous with conversations relating to educational inequality and the implications of socio-economic disadvantage.

So, as directed by government, universities and schools got on with it, attempting to address this 'poverty' of aspiration through various projects, programmes and activities. For universities, this meant investing huge financial resources in activities designed specifically to 'raise aspiration'. And for many schools, the notion became a central concern of their work to support students who were eligible for free school meals (FSM). Activity geared toward improving the educational progression of young people in underserved communities became all about increasing ambition. Big dreams and big hopes for the future. Based on continual messaging by think tanks, regulators and policy makers, educational institutions geared their efforts toward encouraging young people to reach for the stars. To hold aspirations aligned with the highest possible exam grades and study at the most prestigious universities. To move away from home and make their first step toward the middle-class career and lifestyle which awaited them. What wasn't as central to their thinking were its implications for the working-class individuals and communities it was purporting to serve.

While the political discourse has moved on in recent years, with continuing crises linked to Brexit, COVID-19 and numerous global conflicts, the legacy of a 'poverty of aspiration' narrative has been imprinted on our educational systems and structures. You would be hard pressed to find a conversation taking place about inequality in any educational context that doesn't mention aspiration at least once. In many settings, raising aspiration has been a central pillar of work to address unequal opportunity and improve social mobility. It's been written into school values, inserted into people's job titles and for years was heralded by 'prestigious' universities as a crucial instrument in widening access to their institutions.

Given that aspiration raising has become, and continues to be, such a prominent feature of activity to level the educational playing field, it would be fair to assume that it's effective. That a laser focus on aspiration has been the silver bullet, unlocking greater equality of opportunity. Unfortunately, you would be wrong.

Although the first two decades of the 21st century saw a much larger proportion of young people going to university, the gaps in access between those in society who have most and those who have least are still chasmic. According to the university admissions service UCAS,[9] in 2024 37 per cent of 18-year-olds in England had accepted a place to study at university. However, if you were also eligible for FSM, the percentage fell to a little under 20 per cent. If you also happened to be a young man, this figure dropped even further. In 2024, just 15 per cent of young men who were eligible for FSM were accepted to study on an undergraduate university degree. In other words, if you are a young man who may face barriers related to your household income, your chances of making a successful application to university are less than two in ten.

It would be unfair to place these entrenched disparities solely upon the inadequacy of efforts to raise aspiration. Of course, there are many elements which contribute to this stark disparity in educational outcomes and progression, many of which will be highlighted during later conversations. However, within a narrative which repeatedly foregrounds 'poverty of aspiration' as the main reason for inequalities in educational progression, these elements are largely ignored. Given the scale of the issue, we would at least hope to see some evidence that aspiration raising, the much-vaunted antidote to this poverty of ambition, was at least making a difference to pupils' educational outcomes. However, it's very difficult to find.

A key consideration when talking about young people progressing in education is their grades. If school students don't get the qualifications necessary to progress to university, then no matter how high their aspirations are, they won't be going when they turn 18. So, for 'aspiration raising' to support its aim of improving social mobility, it's of vital importance that we see a positive impact from activity on student attainment. However, data to support such a claim are incredibly difficult to find. In a toolkit produced by the Education Endowment Foundation (EEF),[10] a nationally funded 'what works' centre dedicated to breaking the link between family income and educational achievement, a review was conducted of the research and evidence associated with aspiration raising in schools. In their findings, the charity concluded that the evidence base for its impact on students' outcomes was extremely weak. For any of those professionals who have been working relentlessly to support young working-class students in alignment with such an agenda, it's a gut punch. After nearly two decades of efforts to 'raise aspiration', the EEF could not find any clear evidence to suggest that 'aspiration raising' had any direct impact on improving students' attainment. Instead, on their website they wrote:

> Some studies have shown that most young people already have high aspirations, suggesting that much

underachievement results not from low aspiration but from a gap between aspirations and the knowledge, skills, and characteristics required to achieve them. Where pupils do have lower aspirations, it is not clear whether targeted interventions have consistently succeeded in raising their aspirations. Also, where aspirations begin low and are successfully raised by an intervention, it is not clear that an improvement in learning necessarily follows.[11]

What the EEF and many other prominent social and educational researchers including David Gillborn,[12] Diane Reay,[13] Louise Archer[14] and Neil Harrison[15] have found is that lower grades and rates of entry into higher education for students who are eligible for FSM do not come from a 'poverty of aspiration'. Indeed, as highlighted earlier, research suggests that the aspirations of young people who are eligible for FSM may already be high. For those who don't have high aspirations already, it suggests that it is unclear whether having higher aspirations would translate into any improvement in learning.

While it may be a shock to some, with a little more reflection on the nature of aspiration, we can begin to build a picture of why this may be the case. The dictionary definition of aspiration is a 'strong desire, longing or aim'.[16] Synonyms include hankering, craving and yearning. It's a hope for the future. One which may be abstract, intangible and unsupported by the structures necessary to turn it into something more real. Given its meaning, it provides a wobbly foundation on which to base activity to tackle inequality in educational opportunity, especially if evidence suggests that young people's aspirations may already be high. If I think back to my own challenges at school, it took my exclusion and relocation to a much more middle-class setting to provide the conditions necessary for me to pass my exams. Had that not been the case, it's unlikely that any amount of encouragement to 'reach for the stars' would have made up for the lack of tools at my disposal to turn such an ambition into a reality.

However, when it comes to explaining why aspiration raising may be an ill-suited tool to use in education, its ineffectiveness is only one piece of the puzzle. A fuller explanation can be found in the ideas which have underpinned its use since the early 2000s. A model which positions young men and women who may have alternative ideas about their future as 'deficient'.

On the surface, asking young men from working-class communities to dream bigger seems harmless. After all, who wouldn't want a degree from a 'world-leading' university, a nice car, their own house and a high-paying job as a doctor, banker or senior civil servant? But it poses problems. While those working on raising aspiration present the lofty heights of upper-middle-class professions as attainable for all, there's only so much room 'at the top'. Access to the summit is closely guarded through requirements surrounding academic grades, interests and hobbies, social connections and relevant experiences. There is an expectation by admissions tutors, whether explicitly stated or otherwise, that any successful applicant to a 'world-leading' university such as theirs will have these things in abundance.

But what happens to those young men and women who, for whatever reason, don't align themselves to this dream? Who might not get the grades, might not have the experiences or might not have the inclination to follow an educational trajectory aligned with moving away to university? What of those students for whom vocational education is better suited or those who, for numerous reasons, may want to engage with learning in a different way? Are their experiences, skills and ambitions for the future somehow less legitimate because they don't match up with a Hogwarts-style educational experience at a Russell Group university? Well, if you follow the logical outcome of a set of ideals which places a single educational pathway as the ideal, then apparently yes.

The aspiration-raising agenda has set up a false gold standard, one in which the most desirable outcome is excellent performance in exams, leaving home to study at a 'prestigious' university and a 'good' graduate job. Any trajectory which deviates from this 'gold standard' is just a variation of less legitimate. If you study a vocational BTEC qualification rather than studying A levels, less good. If you elect to stay at home and commute to university, less good. If you go to a 'modern university' with slightly lower entry requirements, less good. Within this manufactured hierarchy of future educational destinations, those who are at the bottom of the pecking order are those who choose not to go. In the landscape of aspiration narratives which prize this 'gold standard' of social mobility above all else, the weight of responsibility for its realisation is heaped squarely on to the shoulders of the young men and women in working-class communities where such narratives are most often targeted.

To provide an illustrative example, shortly before the pandemic struck, I made a YouTube video which explained the differences between the level three A level and BTEC qualifications.[17] In England, A levels are broadly viewed as more academic in nature. They are undertaken by students aged 16–18 at schools or in large sixth form colleges. BTEC qualifications have slightly more vocational components and are usually undertaken in large colleges of further education. A report in 2018 by the National Education Opportunities Network also highlighted that students from working-class backgrounds were much, much more likely to take BTEC qualifications than A levels.[18]

Given that students undertaking BTEC qualifications were more likely to experience underrepresentation in higher education, I wanted to find out more. As part of a project for work, I reviewed the prospectuses of the universities which had some of the highest entry requirements in England. I wanted to understand what young men studying BTEC qualifications would need to do to become a student at their institutions. Although at the time, universities with the highest entry tariffs uniformly claimed to accept students holding BTEC qualifications, often information for these students on how to apply was difficult to find. Even though over 100,000 students from the UK applied to university each year holding BTEC qualifications, in many cases the information was nowhere to be found in admissions brochures for 'elite' universities – 100,000 students each year who were notionally eligible to apply for their courses, but the entry requirements were absent from their publicity materials. Conversely, the International Baccalaureate, a qualification undertaken by roughly 4,000 students in the UK annually,[19] featured heavily throughout. It may not surprise you to learn that this post GCSE qualification is predominantly undertaken by students at fee-paying independent schools.

Although these universities claimed to accept BTEC students, information which may help students studying the qualification to make an application appeared to have been withheld at a systemic level. It could be that this was a sheer coincidence. After all, many of the staff working at such universities would never have studied for a BTEC qualification themselves. However, given its widespread nature, I can't help thinking that it may have been less unintentional.

The YouTube video certainly resonated. To date, it has received upward of 30,000 views. Below it are hundreds of comments by students who have watched the video and for whom it struck a chord. Aside from a number commenting on my inability to blink effectively while filming the video, there are several which leave me feeling greatly saddened. In the comments, one young viewer writes 'More people need to speak about these situations. I'm a BTEC student and some people laugh when I tell them.' This comment received the most likes out of any on the video. Whether intentional or not, the message sent to these students is that in studying a BTEC qualification, they are inferior in the eyes of 'prestigious' universities. A notion which is supported by the absence of BTEC qualifications in their prospectuses.

This imagined 'gold standard' of an educational future isn't a harmless notion: it has very real consequences in the minds of working-class young people. Students which, through widening participation programmes, universities claim to want to support. However, very rarely is the lens turned inward by these 'prestigious' institutions to dismantle barriers which are of their own making. Instead, through narratives of aspirational deficit, responsibility is lumped back on to the shoulders of the young people the odds are stacked against.

Turning our attention back to young working-class men, suggestions that they experience a deficit in aspiration also works to devalue any hopes or ambitions they may already hold. Orientations for their future in education and work which have been nurtured through encounters, experiences and conversations with the people whose opinions they hold in highest esteem. Family members and friends, people who work around them and live on the same street. It paints a picture layered with the subtext that because they didn't 'reach for the stars', their lives and occupations lack value. That who they are and what they do isn't aligned with 'success'. It implies that if you happen to be a working-class person from this community, legitimacy can only be bestowed from elsewhere. To gain value, you must escape and set your sights on something completely different. You must 'aim higher'.

Imagine your child coming home from school and being informed that they have spent the day being told that, in order to achieve in life, what you have provided for them as a parent isn't quite good enough. That how and where your family live isn't something that your child should look to emulate. That in fact, the combination of these things has created a deficiency that your child should be aspiring to correct in the future. And what's more, that making this change is the sole responsibility of you and your child. To not buy into these new 'higher' aspirations is to fail.

While the analogy is extreme, it's the implicit message that the aspiration-raising agenda holds. Alongside it being largely ineffectual as a tool to support young working-class men and women to improve educational attainment, it does so in a way which runs counter to the principles of equality and fairness which are so often uttered in the same breath.

So how could we better understand? How could we shift the dial so that work by policy makers and educators serves working-class young men rather than blames them for how they talk, how they dress and where they live? An obvious starting point would be a meaningful recognition that the experiences of young working-class men, and those closest to them, are valued. That their lives, geographies and histories are rich and important. That because of this they have unique experiences which provide them with skills and strengths that other people may not possess. That their ambitions for the future are legitimate, and the goal of educators and policy makers is not to dictate what success means for them but rather to support them in their journey toward a future which is happy, healthy and secure.

What I have just described is called a strengths-based approach. As a concept, it's not new and ties into the work of educational giants such as bell hooks[20] and Paulo Freire.[21] Strengths-based approaches have a long history of use in youth work as a mechanism to build trust and rapport, empowering young people to be active agents in their own lives and communities. They focus on establishing relationships which are not built on hierarchy but mutual respect. However, it is an approach which is often starkly absent from policy conversations surrounding education and equitable access to opportunities for young people, especially in more formal settings such as schools.

So, if we instead took a strengths-based approach, the next step would be finding a way to apply it which is more effective. Alongside its deficit-laden intention, there is very little evidence to suggest that interventions framed around individual aspiration raising are impactful. If we are to escape this aspiration trap, the last thing we want to do is end up creating a whole new set of assumptions which are similarly unproductive. Luckily, there is research out there which allows us to formulate a new understanding, one which embraces the richness and diversity of experiences in working-class communities. Thankfully, it also holds a more substantive base in evidence.

In a paper published by the *British Educational Research Journal* in 2018, academics Neil Harrison and Richard Waller introduced expectations as a potential antidote to the ills associated with discourses founded in 'aspirational impoverishment'.[22] They argued that expectation, if used as part of a strengths-based approach, could be an alternative which is both more equitable and more impactful.

Although it's only a small change, it has the potential to make a big difference. Instead of a focus on students' hopes for the future, expectations are clearer, more tangible. The dictionary describes an expectation as 'the feeling or belief that something will happen'.[23] Not a dream in the abstract, but a concrete assumption that what someone expects to happen will occur. A focus on expectation makes much more sense. It's clearer and more substantive. Importantly, for those working to support young people, it shifts the focus from 'how do we get them to dream bigger?' to 'what support are they going to need for this ambition to become an expectation?'

To use the example of an exam, an aspiration intervention may increase the student's hopes of getting an A. However, if they are currently predicted a C grade, no matter how high that student's ambitions are of getting an A, they are unlikely to realise it through hope alone. If instead the question was 'what can we put into place so that an A is an expectation?', the conversation immediately changes. Rather than a focus on the ambition of the individual student, it shifts to the resources required for the A grade to be the expected outcome. Suddenly it turns to additional tutoring, access to study space at home, additional learning resources and curriculum enrichment opportunities. Rather than the burden of responsibility falling squarely on to the shoulders of the young person, it shifts. The onus falls to those who hold responsibility to support to put those things into place. They know that, in order for an A to be expected, these interventions will need to happen. If they don't, and the student achieves a C, is it the student's fault? No, it was the likely outcome given that the student wasn't given the resources required to improve their attainment. It doesn't heap blame on to the young person for perceived 'deficiencies'; rather it accepts that for the outcome to be different, resources would have been required that in this case weren't available.

Now, if we zoom out to educational inequality, masculinity and working-class boys in a wider context, things get decidedly messier. The 'gold standard' of social mobility and entry into a prestigious university is far more complex than a simple change in an exam grade. To understand it, we need a tool capable of navigating significant nuance and complexity.

In research from the early 2000s, Ball and colleagues conducted a study to formulate a mechanism capable of such navigation.[24] Through their research, they created a typology. It was a template by which the future educational decision making of young people who experience socio-economic disadvantage could be better understood at a deeper level. For the researchers, rather than choices being determined by individual aspiration, they were made by the young people in a continual dialogue with the social, historical and familial context in which the choice was being made. Their decisions didn't float free from these things but were deeply interwoven within experiences linked to place, family and history.

Within the study, participants were split into two categories: *embedded choosers* and *contingent choosers*. For the *contingent choosers* who were largely from working-class backgrounds, going to university involved them becoming a person who was different from the rest of their family and many of their peers. In making the *contingent choice* of an educational future which involved higher education, they chose a path for themselves which differed from nearly everyone they knew. For the *embedded choosers* who were largely from middle-class backgrounds, on the other hand, a future involving university was entirely normal. It was something that most people around them did. The resources required for the young person to frame such a trajectory as an expectation were readily available and within easy reach. It was a natural progression. But, if you happened to be from a working-class background, where university is a *contingent choice*, the prospect looked very different. An imagined future which positioned higher education as the probable destination was fraught with risk. The ambition to attend university amounted to a high stakes gamble which was opaque, unfamiliar and intimidating.

When risk is discussed in the same conversation as university, quite often our minds will jump straight to financial uncertainty and student debt. However, this is just one risk of many facing a young man from a working-class background. If you are from a family and community which holds very little prior experience of higher education, a *contingent chooser*, encouraging the 'gold standard' of higher education participation is asking for a decision to be made between two options. The first is the safe bet. A trajectory through education and into work which doesn't involve university. It's a familiar path followed by numerous friends and family members. Advice and guidance about what to do and where to go can easily be sought and readily given. Intelligence about local jobs, opportunities within the trades or retail and places to study more vocational qualifications are all easily accessible. It might mean a higher chance of financial instability and less security in the long run, but it's known, it's safe, and it's comfortable. Importantly, it also aligns with expectations surrounding what young men 'should do' among peer groups and familial networks. Following this trajectory means there is no sanction for deviating from established masculine expectations.

Conversely, the second option, university, brims with risk. Realising this ambition involves a new educational trajectory outside of the family's experience. It means deferring the opportunity to gain full-time paid employment. It means £9,250 a year tuition fees, student debt and moving away from close friends and family members who support you. While these challenges are bubbling away at the back of your mind about the future in the medium term, you have many more immediate concerns. Discovering ways to access knowledge that you'll need about the application process – especially if you study a BTEC – the complex landscape of entry requirements for certain universities and courses and the types of experiences you would need to make a successful application. None of this is easily available. The process also involves educating your family, who may question the wisdom of your future intentions, on the steps required as much as it does in finding out information on the process for yourself. And if all this wasn't enough, the elephant in the room makes an appearance – even if you do all of this, take all of these steps, tick all of the boxes, it may not be enough. If you are a working-class boy, there is a strong possibility that you might not even get the grades to make it possible. In 2023/24, just 24 per cent of young men who were eligible for FSM attained a grade nine to five (equivalent of grade A*-C) in GCSE maths and english. In other words, their chances of getting the required grades at GCSE to study A levels, let alone go to university, was two in ten.[25]

It's not just a case of ploughing through adversity by 'dreaming bigger'. For young people who don't have easy access to the social, economic and cultural resources aligned with eventual progression to university, it's being asked to fix a car without a toolbox or the manual. When framed in such a manner, who could honestly say that, in their position, they would examine those risks and decide that university was worth the gamble? When laid out, the idea that low rates of university participation for young people from working-class backgrounds can be attributed to an individual lack of aspiration seems quite ludicrous. However, much like the 'gold standard' of educational progression, it has slowly filtered into our understanding of the issue as a society. An unconscious, taken-for-granted assumption that the problem is 'aspiration'. One which, rather than affording opportunity to make meaningful change in the lives of young people, diverts, distracts and is laden with blame. It's a trap that, through the messaging of policy makers, news outlets and public figures, we've collectively fallen into. A snare which has tightened as the years have progressed. If we want to make a real impact on the consequences of inequality in education, we urgently need to extricate ourselves from it.

In reading this chapter, you may have noticed that while there's been a lot of discussion about the consequences of socio-economic inequality on the future educational orientations of working-class young people in a broad sense, for a book which has a specific focus on the experiences of young men, discussion surrounding the role of masculinity in negotiations of socio-economic inequality has been notably absent. The next chapter seeks to address this by continuing to build a depth of knowledge and understanding around the issue, before moving on to the more practical matter of how we can address it in later chapters. It examines how, for young working-class men, negotiating these risks forms a fundamental part of their time in education and beyond.

4

Societal change: boys, inequality and a 'successful' future

Although I've not lived there in years, I still call Burntwood home. If you've never been, I'm not entirely surprised. To give people an idea of its location, the residents of Burntwood spend half their life referring to it by its proximity to Cannock, Lichfield, Walsall or, if all else fails, Birmingham.

At the end of a slip road on the M6 Toll, Burntwood is a small ex-industrial town. In the early 1860s, the quest for black gold reached the area, and communities built around the town worked in the mines. By the end of the century, the population had reached 2,000, and it had become an established presence within the industrial landscape of the West Midlands. Following the closure of the mines nearly a century later, the town's population doubled as the area became an overspill for predominantly working-class families from Birmingham and the Black Country.

Nowadays, Burntwood has a population of around 27,000. With housing development over the last 70 years, it's slowly but steadily grown. That said, it's still a small town. When a McDonald's opened next to the Morrisons back in the early 2010s, it was a very, very big deal.

Now I'm a bit older, I love going back to Burntwood to see my parents. It's the kind of place where everyone knows everyone, or at least knows someone who does. Every year on Christmas Eve, I call my mate, go down the pub around the corner and see the faces of people who have known me for more years than I care to remember. Sitting in the same cosy corner as we did when we were 17, playing pool and reflecting on life since we all last sat around the table.

Within minutes of stepping outside my parents' front door, I can be in the countryside. I spent my childhood traversing the winding narrow lanes that snaked their way toward loftier Lichfield. Summers were devoted to jumping across the stream that runs along the bottom of Gentleshaw Common and climbing the sand dunes which, as a seven-year-old, seemed dizzyingly high.

Burntwood is beautiful. No matter how far away I live, it will always be my home. However, if you were to take your evidence from statistics, your perspective on my hometown might not wholly align with what I've just described. Viewing my parents' postcode through the lens of national data on inequality and deprivation, you would be left with a very different impression.

The postcode of my family home ranks among the top 20 per cent most deprived areas nationally for inequalities related to health, employment and education. Data also suggest that, for young people, progression to higher education is significantly lower than average. To be honest, I find it jarring to talk about my home in these terms. As an area which is 'deprived'. It's certainly not how I, my old friends or anyone down the pub on Christmas Eve would describe it. But at the same time, I can't ignore the fact that the inequalities which the data point to exist. They are there in the number of people, even close friends, I know with significant problems related to physical and mental health. They are present in the lack of opportunities locally for employment and in the educational routes, pathways and orientations which are deemed to be realistic as 'choices'.

Having followed the path through education and work that I have, my story is not normal for a lad from my hometown.

Looking back, there's a reason why it differs. While things weren't always easy, I grew up in a position of comparative privilege. At the age of five, my mum was working as a nurse, and despite entering into the early stages of his challenges with mental ill health and addiction, my dad was working as a teacher. We had two incomes. We were a middle-class family living in a working-class town. As I got older and my dad's battles intensified, things changed. By the time I reached the age of eight, he was oscillating between periods of unemployment and short-term, low-paid jobs: selling mobile phones and double glazing. When I began to develop acute anxiety, my mum cut her hours at work. Essentially, she went part time to look after my dad and me.

However, this period of turbulence doesn't change the fact that both of my parents have been in receipt of opportunities in education and work. These were opportunities that were out of reach for a large number the people I went to school with. It meant that growing up I had easy access to a range of cultural and social resources that I could draw on to align my expectations with continued engagement in education. Two out of my five half brothers and sisters went to study at university while I was growing up. In my family, a future aligned with going to university wasn't something which was alien or abstract – it happened to people who were around me and was part of what my family did.

While there were other things which made my educational progression a challenge, the access to knowledge and social networks gained through my family's educational experiences were always there to draw on.

When I think about my differing familial experiences in terms of my relationships with the people around me, it also made me different. I didn't talk with the same accent as most of my classmates at school, which situated me as a bit of an outsider. I vividly remember being called Alex the Encyclopaedia because of the way I spoke. As an eight-year-old, I was mortified. It's weird – nowadays, I'd happily take being called an encyclopaedia as a compliment, but at the time it wasn't.

Even at that young age, I learned that the best way to stymie such taunting was with my fists. I didn't have a very good track record at winning fights, but that I was willing to get into one made would-be bullies think twice. When compared to the challenges related to serious youth violence in some of our large cities, coming-togethers, confrontations and playground spats in Burntwood were tame. While there was a lot of fighting with fists and feet, this rarely escalated into anything more serious. If drive by 'beating ups' were a thing, Burntwood would have been the home of them.

I didn't realise it at the time, but this feeling of difference, of distance, of not quite fitting in, was tied to something much bigger than the way I spoke. Something which, especially in conversations about masculinity and working-class people, is often wilfully overlooked.

It's to do with how, across generations, we go about our lives in a continual dialogue with the world around us, an unspoken conversation which shapes the way we talk, the way we dress, what we eat and what we do in our spare time. It leads to us feeling at home in certain situations and uncomfortable in others. It influences what we learn, where we live, what we do now and what we might do in the future.

No two conversations are the same. Each person has their own dialogue with the world around them based on their unique collection of knowledge and experiences. Back in primary school, because my dad spoke with a posh accent due to his education in a military boarding school, it meant that the dialogue taking place for me was already different from most of my peers. A difference which I was castigated for at the time, but now I work for a university, is a way of speaking which holds currency as an 'expected' manner of verbal communication. Ironically, I now get told on a regular basis that I have a noticeable West Midlands accent. It turns out that people who work at universities in the South of England tend to speak even posher than my dad. My life growing up in Burntwood and the one I lead now are worlds apart, a social and geographic distance which has been traversed over three decades.

Negotiating the gap between these two worlds is something I now do with relative ease and regularity. However, that feeling of being different, a bit of an outsider, has never quite shifted regardless of my age or experience in navigating the different social contexts. After embarking on the research for my PhD I gradually developed a better understanding of why that may be the case. I found a way, through the knowledge and writing of others, to provide a deeper articulation of the journey I had been on as a young man in education. Moreover, it equipped me with a foundation of knowledge which has underpinned all the work I have undertaken with young men in education since. So, in the coming chapters, I'm going to do my best to summarise the most important bits of what I learned about young working-class men in education and wider society along the way. Hopefully it will save you the cost and effort of undertaking a doctorate yourself while providing you with a set of similar thinking tools to bring to bear on the issue. Once they're established, we'll use them to more deeply understand the challenges facing young working-class men in a contemporary educational context and, most importantly, provide some examples of collective action already being undertaken to level the educational playing field.

The research

The way we talk, the way we act, what we like, what we don't like and what we think about the world around us are shaped by the social conditions in which we exist. That is not to say that, because of those conditions, our future is predetermined, but it would be naive to think that it doesn't have a colossal influence. The term 'working class' is one that is widely used as a catch-all to describe people who don't come from upper- and middle-class backgrounds. In recent years, it is also a term which has caused a fair bit of disagreement among academics and politicians.

It would be quite easy to spend the rest of this book engaging with the numerous debates about 'who working-class people are' and 'what being working class actually means' which populate newspaper articles and social media feeds. Although such discussions are interesting and important, they often also detract from what is in my view a much more important conversation about how to tackle the pervasive implications of stark socio-economic inequality in the UK. While books such as Mike Savage's *Social Class in the 21st Century* provide an excellent insight into how such inequalities are structured,[1] they open a Pandora's box of contestation and debate which contribute little toward the intended purpose of this chapter, or any others in this book.

From this point onward, I will be using the term 'working class' to specifically describe the group of young men which are the book's primary focus. This is not because I want to become embroiled in any of the debates detailed earlier. Rather, it is the only term I am aware of which doesn't position people with less access to cultural, social and economic resources than their more middle-class peers as in some way 'deficient'.

Words like 'disadvantaged', 'poor' and 'deprived' are often used to identify and talk about people who experience socio-economic inequality. They are all terms which I dislike immensely. It leads me to ask: how would you feel being described in that way? Your experiences, your communities, your friendships, your hobbies and interests, all labelled as 'impoverished' because of where and how you grew up. An implicit suggestion that because you grew up in Sunderland, Wolverhampton or Tottenham, your experience of life is somehow diminished; less than ideal.

It's what we do every day. Describing millions of people across the UK with words we'd hate to be turned on ourselves. So, I'm not. Instead, I use the term working class, one which affords an opportunity to celebrate the richness and diversity of experiences across geographies and generations. Of long, proud histories and collective memories spanning centuries. Groups of individuals whose vocations and lives were enmeshed with that of community. While the work was often difficult, dangerous and economically precarious, it carried an inherent pride and sense of worth.

When I use the term to talk about socio-economic inequality in a more contemporary societal context, I do so with a clear intention. I use the term to describe groups of people, who through no fault or choice of their own, feel the consequences of economic inequality most severely. These are inequalities which, according to the Equality Trust,[2] mean that in 2023 the 50 richest families in the UK held more wealth between them than half of the population – 50 people with more money than 34 million combined. When I talk about working-class boys, I'm referring to young people from families who feel the effects of this chasmic divide in the distribution of material resource most keenly.

Research with young working-class men also has a robust history which, when attempting to write a book about it, is a real advantage. For anybody reading this who may have studied an A level in sociology, there's a good chance you will have a vague recollection of Paul Willis's 1977 text *Learning to Labour*.[3] Set in the Black Country, it recounts his research with a group of working-class boys at a school near Wolverhampton. The study set out to unpick how, in the industrial landscape of the West Midlands, working-class boys went on to get 'working-class jobs'. Despite the age of the study, and the language used by Willis make his findings sound a little bit academic and abstract, I feel a deep connection to the research. Not because I am entirely convinced by the presentation of his argument, but because it captures a space and place in time which feels familiar. In *Learning to Labour*, Willis interprets the words and actions of young men who grew up just a few miles from my childhood home.

Within the text, he describes two distinct groups among the working-class boys he engaged with, 'the lads' and 'the ear' oles'. He presents the culture of 'the lads' as one in which they deliberately failed in education. Not because they weren't smart, but because they saw school as having little relevance to the menial work in factories and refineries that awaited them. Instead, he describes how, through engagement in practices which constituted 'having a laff', including drinking, smoking, disrupting lessons and messing around, 'the lads' gained status by their investment in an anti-school subculture. For Willis, 'the lads' were a group in which macho, aggressive behaviour and instances of casual sexism and racism were the defining feature.

Although located nearly two decades before my own journey through education, there are significant chunks of Willis's analysis which resonate with my experiences as a teenager, especially the treatment of those who deviated from this imposed set of masculine ideals. Willis describes how these young men were derided by their peers as 'ear' oles'. Not only did 'the lads' not like school but there was active disdain for anyone who was seen to deviate from their view. Behaviours which were seen as conforming to the institution were positioned as effeminate, weak and undesirable. In the text, Willis reflects that what drove the disdain was 'not so much that they supported the teachers, rather they supported the idea of what teachers represent'.[4] For 'the lads', the notion that anyone would *want* to conform at school was absurd enough to warrant ridicule.

Willis articulates the culture celebrated by 'the lads' in school as activity to lay the foundation for a transition into a working-class job as a 'breadwinner', the sole provider of a family's income. A position which, in the industrialised landscapes of the early 1970s, was inextricably tied into the perceived worth and value of masculinity, especially if you happened to be working class.

In many ways, *Learning to Labour* is a text which marked the end of the industrial era in England. Some 20 years after the book's publication, Willis wrote that he 'caught "the lads" in *Learning to Labour* at the end of what was perhaps the last golden period of working-class cultural coherence and power in a fully employed Britain'.[5] The study took place at a point in time which marked the final days before the commencement of an economic shift which resulted in large-scale deindustrialisation across the Black Country and much of the West Midlands. Initiated under the Conservative government of Margaret Thatcher, following the publication of *Learning to Labour*, deindustrialisation dramatically shifted the social and economic fortunes of the region. A change which, as documented by Willis himself, significantly altered the landscape of opportunity for working-class employment across the region.

With his focus on 'the lads' nearly half a century ago, Willis engaged with a group of young men that neatly fit into stereotypical notions of what a working-class boy 'looks like'. Following the publication of his book, it shot to academic fame. To date, an edition by Routledge published in 2017 has over 22,000 citations on Google Scholar, having become a seminal text within sociology curriculums and university reading lists. In school classrooms and university seminar rooms, the work foregrounds a specific type of working-class masculinity as that which is most common: 'the lads'.

But what of 'the ear' oles'? That group who didn't fit snugly into stereotypical narratives surrounding how working-class boys act, what they like and how they learn? A group who engaged educationally, setting their sights on education and employment more commonly associated with middle-class students. Dismissed by 'the lads' as 'wimps' for not modelling aggressive behaviour and casual sexism, 'the ear' oles' were likely to leave school with academic qualifications and enter 'white collar' jobs in teaching or office work. In other words, they were a group who did not fit neatly into preconceived ideas about what a working-class boy 'should' be. Yet their lives and experiences were overlooked.

Although it's a piece of research which has had a profound impact on the way we think about young working-class men, both in education and in wider society, there are some rather large holes in Willis's analysis. Not only in his privileging of 'the lads' but also the binary nature of a discussion which sets 'the lads' against 'the ear' oles'. It's a very black and white way of looking at things, especially in a world which is characterised by shades of grey. This 'determinism' is something which, ten years later, Phillip

Brown sought to address in his book *Schooling Ordinary Kids*.[6] Currently sitting at 500 citations on Google Scholar, Brown's research wasn't received quite as sensationally as the work of Willis. Given the discussion that took place in the previous chapter on aspiration, this may not come as much of a surprise. Willis's characterisation of 'the lads' plays into a very particular view of working-class young men in compulsory education. It positions their presence in the classroom as problematic and their identities as deficient when considered against the codes of conduct they are expected to adhere to. In other words, 'the lads' fall very neatly into stereotypical, largely middle-class assumptions about who working-class boys are. In doing so, it provides an ongoing justification for those who wish to frame their very existence in educational spaces as 'the problem'.

What it doesn't do, however, is offer an accurate reflection of my own experience in education or that of many of my working-class friends. While at my first school there were a few young working-class men whose attitudes and behaviours aligned closely to Willis's description of 'the lads', numerically speaking they were a very loud, very small, minority. Most of the young men I went to school with weren't 'lads' or 'ear' oles'. Their backgrounds, experiences and attitudes toward education were much more diverse and nuanced. Some were shy, some were funny and some of them wanted nothing more than to fly under the educational radar There were lads who were really clever but spent their life trying to hide it, and others who struggled more academically but quietly worked their socks off to avoid being labelled as 'thick'. Not an aggressive, anti-authoritarian mob, but a bunch of ordinary kids who were trying to figure out their place in the world and what it meant to be a young man.

It is for this reason that Brown's work is important. Rather than providing fuel for assumptive narratives which seek to gather young working-class men into a homogenous blob, it took a wider view. The research sought to understand how a broad spectrum of working-class young men found their way in education and work during the turbulent economic period of the late 1980s. He argued that there was an invisible majority of working-class students who 'neither left their names engraved in honours boards, nor gouged them into the top of classroom desks'.[7] They weren't 'lads', they weren't 'ear' oles', they were normal working-class kids. It was on the educational orientations of this group that Brown wished to shine a light.

Set in an urban area of South Wales with a proud industrial heritage, his study surveyed around 450 young working-class men and women. Following the survey up with interviews, he set out to understand what a typical school experience looked like for the working-class participants involved. He argued that their expectations for the future in education and work were dictated by three specific frames of reference. There were those who were concerned with 'getting in' to work as quickly as possible; for these students, school held little concern or meaning. In contrast, there were those for whom 'getting out' was a priority. These students held themselves as distinctive to their classmates and were concerned with engaging in activity to pursue careers outside of those which could be considered the 'norm' in their working-class community.

Finally, there were a significant number of young men he described as the invisible majority. Young men that were simply concerned with 'getting on'. For this group of 'ordinary' students, the priority was simply a transition into secure, well-paid work within their local working-class community. They weren't at either ends of Willis's 'lads' and 'ear' oles' binary but rather fluctuated depending on circumstance. They struck a balance based on their own educational experiences and individual frames of reference. Brown argues that rather than their behaviour being easily grouped into two categories, it was dependent on their own aspirations, intentions for the future and individual circumstance. These 'ordinary' students struck a balance, resisting education in areas they didn't find interesting or relevant and accommodating those they did.

However, he also argued that all of this operated within a set of overarching rules which were dictated by the young men's social and economic context. In other words, if the local economy generated enough working-class jobs for school leavers, they had an established route into employment. If those rules didn't change, schooling was relatively successful in mediating the conflicts and contradictions negotiated by many working-class kids in the classroom. However, due to the economic shift that accompanied deindustrialisation, he argued that this delicate ecosystem had been disrupted. It fractured local employment opportunity and, with it, the chances of local young men progressing into good 'working-class' jobs.

The research by Willis and Brown charts the early impact of the seismic economic change that came with deindustrialisation and Thatcher's neoliberal agenda. Through the privatisation of much of the country's previously state-owned industries, Thatcherism set the country on a new trajectory. It was one which saw opportunities for 'good working-class' jobs in industries such as coal, steel and manufacturing disintegrate. Today, the legacy of change is still felt in a world which looks very different for young men in those towns and cities which used to form the United Kingdom's industrial heartland.

By 2016, around the time I was beginning my doctoral research, academics Mac an Ghaill and Haywood argued that the societal context surrounding working-class men had changed significantly.[8] Following the period of large-scale deindustrialisation and economic transition, the researchers highlighted how inequalities faced by predominantly White, working-class communities in towns and cities with an industrial heritage had slipped off the bottom of the list of governmental priorities. However, with the country facing new economic turmoil instigated by the 2008 financial crisis and exacerbated by Brexit, those same communities began to re-emerge within the political and media discourse. However, when they did so, it was in a very different way. Due to the complex history of the communities and their relationship to the socio-economic upheaval of the preceding three decades, a simple analysis of their experience as victims of material circumstance in an unequal society now held little power to explain what was going on.

Social conditions during the period had changed dramatically and so had the worldview of those in power. Mac an Ghaill and Haywood argue that because the defining characteristics of working-class communities had become detached from industrial jobs in steel, rubber or mining as the industries disintegrated, they were replaced by a new narrative of who working-class men were, aligned to a worldview dominated by free markets and individual choice. A social and economic transformation instigated by the

Conservative government under Thatcher. Within this new status quo, consumption was king. Rather than being defined by their work within an industrial economic context, working-class men found themselves being described by where they went, what they drank and what they bought in the shops. Practices such as drinking alcohol, watching football and aggressive sexualities became synonymous with working-class men. In this new ideological landscape, rather than there being a sense of pride and heritage associated with working-class masculinity, their likes, interests and dispositions became undesirable characteristics within a policy narrative which framed them as lacking.

It meant that, growing up as a teenager in the early 2000s, people who lived on the estate around the corner from me were increasingly being denigrated as scallies,[9] scroungers and chavs.[10] Rather than an understanding of working-class people as individuals with a proud history of contributing to the country's economic infrastructure, the narrative changed. Working-class communities increasingly became the subject of ridicule, scorn and stigma. Politicians and newspaper articles decried individuals from these communities as tax dodgers and benefit cheats, while TV shows such as *Shameless* and *The Jeremy Kyle Show* simultaneously handed a permission slip to the wider British public in making working-class communities 'legitimate' subjects of middle-class mockery and disdain.

In a contribution to a 2009 publication called *Who Cares about the White Working Class?* by the Runnymede Trust,[11] eminent sociologist Diane Reay argues that the issue is far more nuanced and complex than a simple story of 'cultural deficiency' could ever account for. In the chapter, which engages with the experience of White working-class students in schools, she argued that young men bought with them a collective memory of educational marginalisation and subordination which spanned generations. Reay contended that the young people weren't 'choosing' to fail because they lacked drive, ambition or aptitude. Instead, it was because they carried the negative educational experiences of their parents and grandparents with them into the classroom. Back in Burntwood when I was growing up, my friends from home and I did not float around in a bubble which isolated our educational ambitions and future orientations from our friends and family members. Rather we engaged in a dialogue with these trusted advisors to accrue reliable, first-hand knowledge about what we might expect from life both inside and outside the school gates.

It is a very simple, yet very important point. How likely a working-class young person may be to actively engage in education cannot be effectively understood without first truly understanding who they are, where they come from and the influence of historical experience on their here and now. In my case, I was lucky: the continued engagement that my parents had with education made my own progression to university a very real possibility. But for many of my friends that was not the case. With parents and grandparents who had been systematically let down by education, advice and guidance came from an understanding of education as a place of risk. Rather than it being a 'passport to a bright future', they viewed formal educational settings with a suspicion reinforced by their own experiences of harm, stigma and marginalisation. From their perspective, school was a woefully inadequate source of the necessary equipment to combat the inequalities they experienced. Instead, as highlighted by Reay, they clung on to the working-class values of leaving school at the earliest possible opportunity and getting a respectable job in the trades. Rather than their identities being characterised by where they went, what they drank and what they bought, they were negotiated in a continual dialogue with the socio-economic upheaval of the past 30 years. The challenges they faced were deeply embedded within their social histories, something which, despite the best efforts of government and the media at the time, could not be eradicated.

In an attempt to grapple with what this 'collective memory' meant for young working-class men transitioning from education into work in a more contemporary context, Ward researched the lives of young men in the South Wales Valleys.[12] Published in 2015, his research explored how the working-class community's social history played out in the experiences of young men who were navigating the transition to adulthood. Shining a light on a future which was negotiated in a continual dialogue with their social networks and the place they lived, Ward sought to develop a deep understanding of what it meant to be a young working-class man from an old mining town in South Wales.

Based on deep qualitative research over a period of two and a half years, his study involved numerous interviews and time spent with a group of young working-class men. During this time, he built a rich picture of their lives, experiences and orientations for the future. Similar to Willis's and Brown's work some 30 years earlier, he categorised the young men into three groups: 'The Valley Boiz', 'The Geeks' and 'The Emos'. Holding similarities to Willis's 'lads', 'The Valley Boiz' displayed a specific version of masculinity, closely tied to the industrial past of the locality. This group was perhaps most closely aligned with dominant, stereotypical notions of working-class masculinity. 'The Geeks', however, displayed a more studious version of masculinity. The defining characteristic for this group was academic advancement and an interest in comic books, technology and reading. However, Ward reflects that the interests of 'The Geeks' sometimes placed them at risk of becoming a target for bullies. The final group, 'The Emos', displayed alternative versions of masculinity which were prominent at the time within the emo subculture. However, while adopting different ways of dressing and preferences for music, they also adopted practices such as binge drinking which reinforced the dominant forms of masculinity which were prominent within their social networks in the working-class town.

While at first glance this may seem like a more contemporary take on the research of Willis and Brown, there is a key difference. Ward's study engages with a fluidity and complexity within the experiences of the young working-class men that within the earlier studies was notable by its absence. Capturing a snapshot of teenage life at a time when I was transitioning into adulthood myself, it also feels very familiar. I wouldn't go as far as saying I embraced the 'emo' subculture as heavily as the participants in Ward's study, but the sounds of Dashboard Confessional, Fallout Boy and Taking Back Sunday certainly featured on my iPod Nano. What I did feel acutely, however, was the uncertain nature of my position as a young man.

The consequences of the substantial socio-economic change imposed upon the region which the study illustrates so eloquently are familiar to me. Describing the tensions and contradictions which were a constant companion to the boys' experience in education, Ward captures the messiness and fluidity of life as a young working-class man. He speaks of how, at times, 'The Valley Boiz' displayed behaviours which contested stereotypical forms of working-class masculinity, while at others 'The Geeks' displayed cracks in their studious personas. Such cracks, he argued, were illustrative of the difficulties faced by 'The Geeks' in aligning their educational ambitions toward becoming geographically and socially mobile. It was a trajectory that fell outside of what was 'expected' but allowed them to realise their aspirations of studying at university. In describing these tensions, Ward talks about the participants' negotiations of identity as a 'chameleonisation'. That is to say that the way young men engaged in masculine behaviour across the categories wasn't fixed. It evolved in a constantly changing relationship with the social, geographic and material conditions of their existence. He argued that the new times the participants found themselves in demanded new ways of being young men.

Although the concept of what it meant to be a working-class man from South Wales had altered over time, the localised versions of working-class masculinity reminiscent of Willis's 'lads' still existed, despite the complete collapse of coal mining in the area. Ward's study argued that just because times have changed in the occupational sense, those symbolic associations with industry and working-class manhood haven't simply disappeared. He illustrates the tensions between old and new. A fragile negotiation between the scarce opportunity for employment in an ex-mining town in South Wales and the forms of masculinity associated within the region's legacy of industrial, working-class employment. The study demonstrates how masculinity is bound within the geographic and social histories of communities. Contexts which, for working-class young men, diminish the likelihood of them fully engaging in practices associated with the pursuit of educational 'success'.

Steve

I spent the early months of my doctoral research in a time warp. Day after day, wading through a sea of academic books, journal articles and reports in search of studies like those mentioned in this chapter. Slowly but surely, I drew together pieces of a fragmented puzzle which led to a deeper understanding. A way to conceptualise and articulate the experiences of young working-class men in education that went beyond simplistic notions rooted in their perceived deficiencies. With each book chapter and journal article, I felt myself moving toward an explanation which was deeper and more meaningful. During this time, Twitter was my best friend. Each time I read an article I found interesting, I searched for the names of the authors to see if they had an account. Back in 2017, this was how I found Professor Steven Roberts.

Originally from England, Steve currently works at Monash University in Australia and is a prolific scholar. During his comparatively short tenure as an academic, he's authored over 90 publications including multiple books, chapters and journal articles about the experiences of young working-class men and their transition into adulthood. However, more than that, he is a hugely supportive colleague and is someone I respect and admire immensely. With dark, swooshy hair and a roguish grin, he isn't exactly what might spring to mind when you think of a stereotypical university professor. Steve is young, charismatic and remarkably normal.

Like many of the individuals I've spoken with for this book, he's also from a working-class background and does some great work as a member of the Alliance of Working-Class Academics alongside my friend and colleague Dr Craig Johnston.[13] In 2021, having cited Steve's research heavily in my PhD, I read a blog he authored which spoke about his experience navigating domestic violence as a young man.[14] It was raw, personal and at times incredibly difficult to read. Steve's words had an openness and vulnerability which are rarely found in academic circles. Upsetting and inspiring in equal measure, the blog shone a light on just why he cares so much about his work. Like many young working-class men, Steve took a break from education before eventually enrolling at university as a mature student. Due to his mix of personal experience and discipline-specific expertise, he was right at the top of my list of people to have a conversation with about masculinity, inequality and the educational transitions of young men. So, at 2 am on a chilly winter's night in 2022, we braved the time difference and spoke at length about his experiences, his values and how they aligned with his work. We talked about how his journey into adulthood shaped his research interests and ignited a commitment to social justice. About how his experiences afforded him the opportunity to develop a critical consciousness around gender and inequality which, as an academic, is one of the most significant tools he brings to bear. He reflected that a critical point in the development of this consciousness came during his time working in the retail sector immediately after leaving school:

> I guess being a teenager and one of my stepdads giving me a hard time about working in a shop instead of doing manual labour. Saying 'ohh yeah it must be really hard to stand up and fold jumpers all day'. Like this kind of sledging, like little banter I suppose; but trying to put me down a bit as well. It was driven by making sense of that experience, which I assumed must be common. But it was not very visible. Instead, what we had was tons of research talking about working-class people in heavily industrialised places from the past. As I mentioned in my book, if you go to any of the major city centres in the North of England, even in the industrial powerhouses like Newcastle and Manchester, they have enormous service sectors. Where were these service sectors and the many, many, young people, young adults that work in them. Where were their stories in the research?

Alongside his early forays into paid employment, Steve also identified two experiences which were instrumental components of his developing ambitions in educational research. First, he explained that, as a child, there was a strong sense of political consciousness within his community. Hailing from an ex-mining town, Steve was born into a family which was heavily engaged with the trade union movement. They were also anti-apartheid activists, supporting the campaign for Nelson Mandela's release from prison in South Africa in the late 1980s. His second reason, however, was a lot more personal. Steve's experience of physical abuse as a young man had a profound impact on him. Looking back, he explains how, alongside a visceral understanding of the implications of trauma for young working-class men, it instilled within him an intense dislike of violence:

> I've always rejected it, and it stems from quite significant, quite severe interactions with men who have beaten me up really badly and, you know ... I've witnessed men's violence in such a profound way, and I guess it could have tipped me one way or the other. But it tipped me towards not wanting to; not wanting to be that kind of man.
>
> They set me on a path to not want to be them. I don't know if it's unusual or not. I know that the go-to response is that people think that if, you're a victim of violence – especially as a boy – if you're the victim of gendered domestic violence, then you're likely to reproduce that behaviour. I think my experience was the opposite.

Although these experiences were clearly intensely traumatic, rather than being a fire which trapped him in a burning building, they did the opposite. He used them as rocket fuel, aligning memories from childhood with a fierce desire to make a difference. Using that deep personal knowledge as a foundation on which to build depth of understanding, Steve uses his research to explore new possibilities for young men from working-class backgrounds. Ways to disrupt intergenerational relays of trauma and violence and support others to do the same.

However, when it came to the wider pressures of 'expected' behaviours for young working-class men, on his journey to adulthood Steve wasn't immune to the allure of actions, attitudes and behaviours which he now looks back on with regret. Like the young men in the research discussed earlier, he felt a strong pull to engage in the 'expected' behaviours for a young man in a deindustrialised working-class community: 'I did engage in some laddish behaviours that you know that I'm not proud of at all, and we want to encourage boys to try and step away from. But, you know, that masculine discourse was prevalent and pervasive.' While there was pressure to engage in behaviours that Steve suggests were linked to dominant masculine expectations within his community, the influence of his mum and the other women in his life constituted foundations on which he built his life and future career:

> The foundational moments for me to reflect and build from came from the influence of my mum and other women in my life. As I say, the converse of that is that the men who basically who were my dads to all intents and purposes. There were a series of them who were violent towards my mum, myself and my siblings.

When considering Steve's experience against my own, we have a lot in common. Involvement in violence and the pressure to engage in certain behaviours to fit in with what was expected. Eventually reaching a critical juncture where the harm it was doing to myself and others was recognised. Of course, there are also many, many differences in our stories, but these elements built a sense connection and understanding. A shared purpose. For both of us, our 'adverse experiences' have acted as a catalyst to drive forward the work we do. A way to process the trauma and provide a soothing salve to some of the hurt. While, as we have discussed at length, the risks that young working-class men face when embarking upon their own journey to, through and out of education are almost too numerous to count, in both of our cases we made it by drawing strength and purpose from our role models. Interestingly, in both of our cases these role models happened to be our mums.

Steve's capacity to deeply understand the implications of inequality and domination came from living them. It was clear that these experiences forged a desire to use his research to bring about change for a significant proportion of young men who may have encountered similar trauma. But in order to articulate the nuanced and complex role of gender and social class within his experiences, he needed a set of tools capable of providing a deeper understanding of society's role in shaping the experiences of young working-class men. So, he set out to do just that. Having spent the last 20 years as an academic specialising in social class and masculinity, he understands better than most the tensions and conflicts which are inherent within his work:

> I think it's trying to balance a focus on the way that working-class people have been dominated, but not ruling out any of the opposite. Really articulating the ways that working-class boys and men can negotiate and enact masculinity in a way that is harmful to themselves and to others. The other side of that is increasingly featuring in my work. To think about the way that the lives of those same dominant and dominated people can be sites of progress and change. Increasingly I'm drawing on bell hooks' work with my colleague Karla Elliott to think about these margins as sites of progress. I'm trying to balance all those things, working to understand how inequality plays out in the lives of young working-class men, but not doing so in a way which renders groups which have previously been underrepresented in research as being completely innocent and benign.

Through his words, Steve lands on an issue which is fundamental to understanding the problems linked to masculinity, social inequality and what we can do about it. The fact that a duality exists. One which looks very different given the levels of social, educational, economic and cultural opportunity you are privileged with having access to. The research discussed earlier demonstrates how working-class boys and men may experience inequality linked to their social class, geography and history. Indeed, through the work of Willis, Brown and Ward, we see how the world of working-class men is constantly shaped and reshaped in a continual dialogue with their geographies, histories and communities. Contexts which, due to shifting socio-economic sands, mean that for many, opportunities in education, work and wider society, are starkly absent.

But this does not mean that working-class young men are without agency. They are not just crisp packets in the wind being blown around by the forces of government policy and socio-economic change. Nor are stereotypical tropes of violence and aggression associated with men completely fabricated. If they were, we wouldn't have the statistics related to violence against women or rates of entry into the criminal justice system that we do. As Steve highlights within his own negotiation of domestic violence as a child, people have agency to make choices in any situation. It is possible, and sadly all too common, for young men to be the victims of systemic inequality while at the same time enacting masculinity in a way which does great harm to themselves and others around them. It is possible to simultaneously be dominated and dominant depending on the context and the power you hold within it. These things aren't an either/or binary. They sit uncomfortably together.

Steve's research into gender, masculinity and inequality grapples with these contradictions and paradoxes. He doesn't attempt to frame the boys and men he engages with as actors who are innocent and benign but instead attempts to show how in a world which is messy, complex and contradictory, we can make change for the better. Drawing on the work of feminist theorist, educator and author bell hooks, he seeks to examine how sites of domination and oppression between genders can be transformed. Alongside his colleague and widely published academic Dr Karla Elliott,[15] Steve seeks to explore how these settings can morph into sites of progress. Working with men and boys on the social margins, Steve and his contemporaries are looking for a new narrative of working-class masculinity. One characterised by hope.

The work of Steve and many other researchers like him shines a light on how, for working-class young men, the world is a markedly different place from that which was discussed in Willis's *Learning to Labour* in the 1970s. We have seen how social and economic upheaval played a fundamental role in shaping the dispositions and future orientations of young men on their journey through education and into work. Steve's research provides us with a starting point, a way to begin to grapple with our understanding of how masculinity, and the expectations associated with it, play out for working-class young men. At a time when mines, steelworks and rubber factories have been replaced with Uber, Amazon fulfilment centres and TikTok, it provides a beacon of understanding of how we can begin to navigate masculinity and inequality in a new and different world.

5

Working-class boys in London:
the capital's overlooked lads

There is a significant omission in the previous chapter. For the last 7,000 words of this book, we've been discussing the experience of working-class young men through a narrow lens, one which provides exclusive attention to predominately White, deindustrialised, working-class communities in regions such as the Midlands, the North of England and South Wales. But what of the other young working-class men? Those who may reside in the UK's bigger cities like London, Birmingham or Manchester? If we are going to get to grips with what being a young working-class man in education means, then we need to widen our gaze, embracing a diversity of experiences which come with differing locations, cultures and social histories.

As a White, now middle-class man, it is unlikely I'd be sanctioned for overlooking knowledge and experiences which don't come from White, middle-class sources. In fact, it happens all too often. And as someone from a small, predominantly White working-class town in the West Midlands, I could be let off by arguing that I don't have the required foundation of lived experience to speak about such experiences with any sense of legitimacy. I don't know what it's like to grow up in London, and I will certainly never be able to understand what it's like to navigate our educational systems and structures as a young working-class Black man. All of these things, however, make it more important that they are discussed.

The feeling of discomfort that comes with doing something when, at the time, it would be easier not to, has been a characteristic of many of the more difficult decisions I've made in later life. As a young man, it was the opposite. I often gave precedence to 'easy but wrong' over 'hard but right'. Whether it was in a choice to throw my lot in with the bullies at school, treat people I loved badly or blame someone else for problems that were in my power to resolve, I chose the easy path.

While the choice I made to write about life for working-class men is very different, it is also similar. If I had chosen not to write this chapter, I wouldn't have been told off – in fact, there would probably be very little in the way of formal repercussions. But it wouldn't be the right thing to do. Once again, we'd have another book which only gave voice to the knowledge, lives and experiences of one dominant demographic, in a society which holds an amazing richness and diversity of experiences. I write this chapter in the knowledge that I don't have all the equipment necessary to offer the depth of truth or understanding that it deserves. Such knowledge would only come from experience living with inequalities which, as a young White boy from Burntwood, didn't feature within my childhood or teenage years. However, omitting it would be the far greater sin. So, this chapter begins with a reflection on what I've learned from encounters with someone who is far more of an authority in this area than I could ever be. The scholar, grime artist and activist Akala.

On a sunny spring evening in 2018, I was sat in a lecture hall at Birmingham City University attending an event for the launch of Akala's new book, *Natives: Race and Class in the Ruins of Empire*.[1] In his introduction, Akala highlighted how, within government and media discourse, the term 'working class' is one which is only used to segment White people on socio-economic terms. He explained that if you were a young working-class Black man from London, the political and media discourse was not kind enough to differentiate you based on the money you had in your bank account. You could be unemployed and live in a bedsit, or running a private medical practice on Harley Street, it didn't matter. What mattered was the colour of your skin. Within mainstream public conversation, it appeared the luxury of being described as working class was reserved for a select few – those from the predominately White communities located in the same deindustrialised towns and cities we discussed in the last chapter.

In reports of knife crime and serious youth violence, never would the newsreaders specify that it happened between 'two groups of Black working-class youths'. Instead, these young men were simply described as 'Black'.

At the time, I was about a third of the way through my PhD research, which sought to examine the educational experience of White working-class young men in the West Midlands. As someone who didn't have a background in sociology and Critical Race Theory before starting the doctorate, the event put what I thought I knew about what I was researching through an intellectual tumble dryer. I came away from the visit to Birmingham with far more than I expected. It was the beginning of a completely new understanding of the intersection between race, class and socio-economic inequality.

Months later, I was sitting on the sofa watching mid-morning television while I procrastinated over something more important that I was meant to be doing and witnessed something quite incredible. Piers Morgan actually *agreeing* with someone. What was even more extraordinary was the person he was agreeing with. While Good Morning Britain doesn't feature regularly in my roster of daytime televisual entertainment, my interest piqued when, as I was flicking through the channels, Morgan's face appeared announcing the MOBO award-winning artist, Akala, as an upcoming guest. Armed with the knowledge that a liberal left-leaning worldview wasn't the position which had established Morgan as a prominent figure within the British mainstream media, I set down the TV remote in anticipation of the verbal mid-morning slugfest which was about to unfold.

Opening the interview in characteristic fashion,[2] Morgan started the discussion on serious youth violence in London with the following question: 'We get told time and again: "Look, it's all very well you middle-class White people telling us what the problem is, right?" Well, you're not middle class and you're not White. What is the problem, and how do we deal with this?' So Akala did. He outlined to Morgan exactly what the problem was, and how it could be addressed. Pointing out that, while there was still an element of personal responsibility, the social indicators of violent crime – relative poverty, masculinity, exposure to domestic violence and a lack of education – among young working-class street gangs had remained consistent for the past 200 years. With admirable levels of calm and eloquence, he explained to the bullish host that there were fairly obvious solutions. Highlighting that 'knife crime' had been a racial buzzword in its association with young Black men, he drew on the example of Glasgow. Once dubbed the most violent city in Europe, Akala described how Glasgow's public health approach to tackling the issue had seen a dramatic reduction in youth violence. He explained how, in a city which had a higher murder rate than London, a holistic, inter-agency approach, underpinned by early intervention, yielded results. It worked to such a significant extent that, of the murders of teenagers in the UK in 2017, none of them occurred in Scotland. Akala spoke of the importance of working with families and communities, diverting them from crime. Within communities experiencing high levels of poverty, 'it doesn't take a rocket scientist to work out that good education, good jobs and access to mental health services led to positive outcomes'. With an example of such effective practice in existence in the UK, he argued, why was there all this hand wringing and suggestions of completely different policies for places like London, Birmingham and Manchester?

The line of questioning continued to revolve around race, with Morgan asked a question with specific reference to statistics in London:

> This is predominantly a problem of young, Black teenage boys who are members almost exclusively of gangs attacking each other so that the perpetrators and the victims appear to be almost exclusively young Black men. Do you think there is a racial element to that in terms of any cultural issues, racial issues, or do you think it's the same problem we had in Glasgow where they were White, but actually the race part of this is something that we might look at the statistics and think it's a Black problem when it's not?

In response, Akala spoke to the numerous geographic regions in England which had higher rates of murder than London. Providing examples of horrendous instances of knife attacks in

Southampton, York and Oxfordshire, where, all of a sudden, the race of the perpetrator appeared to become unimportant. It seemed strange to Akala that race was only mentioned in relation to Black young people in London.

However, he went on to assert that in one limited sense, race may be important. For a very particular demographic of young Black men, at a very particular stage of their lives, there may be a degree to which a level of psychological self-hatred or contempt for themselves is projected on to other people. But, he went on to explain, the Black-on-Black violence paradigms are never spoken about as a model of psychological self-hatred. As one which is inflicted upon individuals by systemic racism. Instead, it is mobilised with the opposite intention. In a similar way to broad-brush presentations of young working-class young men in education as anti-authoritarian and aggressive, the Black-on-Black violence narrative is used to lump an incredibly diverse section of the population together under the label of 'Black'. This provides the ridiculous impression that Black school teachers, Black doctors, Black lawyers, Black Premier League footballers, Akala's grandmother and Ozwald Boateng are all at equal risk of falling into violent crime in a similar way to young working-class men – the individuals to which these narratives are *actually* referring.

Furthering his point, Akala gave the example of paedophiles, illustrating that even though thousands of White middle-aged men are convicted of such crimes, it's self-evident that not all White middle-aged men are paedophiles. Turning his focus, he presented the other side of the coin, where Black boys overachieve in education:

> Is race offered as an explanatory factor? For example, British, Ghanaian and Nigerian boys on free school meals – so the poorest sector – academically outperform and are more likely to go to university than similarly poor White mixed race and Black English kids whose grandparents came from the Caribbean. The four youngest children in Britain to ever take GCSEs are all Black. Ramarni Wilfred a young Black boy from east London, has a higher IQ than Einstein. Young Black men are more disproportionately represented

in professional football than any other area of British life, with all of the consequences and implications that has for their contribution to the tax base. So it's almost as if a Black person does something negative and the entire so-called Black community is to blame. But a Black person does something positive, and they suddenly regain their humanity and their right to be viewed as an individual.

When combined with the fact that almost half of the young people entering the criminal justice had been in care, or that almost half of the prison population had been expelled from school, Akala points to the weakness and frankly absurdity of an explanation for serious youth violence in London which centralises race as the important issue.

The quotes provided in this chapter are only snippets of the interview, and it's well worth watching the whole exchange on YouTube. Contrary to an agenda which sought to racialise the issue of serious youth violence, laying the blame squarely at the feet of young Black men, Akala shifts the viewfinder to focus on the impact of socio-economic inequality. Rather than accepting a narrative which framed young people in London as a special case, a case where the causes of violence were somehow unique or different from those influencing young men across the rest of the UK, he identifies the commonality between them. Whether it's in London, Glasgow, Nottingham, Manchester or Birmingham, the likelihood of young men engaging in serious youth violence has a lot to do with intergenerational experiences of socio-economic inequality and almost nothing to do with the colour of their skin.

However, while that is undoubtedly true, it is also the case that London is very different from Newcastle, in the same way as Norwich is very different from Birmingham. So, if we move past those lazy tropes peddled about serious youth violence and examine some of the more complex indicators linked to masculinity and social history for young working-class men in London, what can we learn? How, given the foundation of knowledge built over the preceding chapters, can we further develop our collective understanding of masculinity, inequality and its relationship with space, places and histories? Are the experiences of young working-class men in London significantly different from those of young men in deindustrialised towns and cities in the North of England? And if so, what do we need to understand?

In answering these questions, my life and experience growing up in a small Midlands town leave me woefully ill equipped to pass comment on life as a young working-class man growing up in London. Burntwood has a population of 27,000 people. London has a population of 9 million. In fact, if you combined the number of London's coffee shops and fast-food restaurants, there would be one for each married couple in my hometown to use exclusively. My hometown also isn't what you would describe as multicultural. In the 2021 census, just 3.7 per cent of Burntwood's residents did not report their ethnicity as White British. In terms of a physical space, it was as close to the opposite of the day-to-day experiences of a teenage Londoner as you can imagine. In light of this, I reached out to Owen Thomas, an individual who, through his own lived and professional experience, was far better equipped to engage in reflections surrounding class, inequality and masculinity in London.

Owen

Hailing from the heart of old industrial Bermondsey, Owen works for an organisation called Future Men. Based in London, Future Men was founded around a single issue: men and masculinity. Established in 1988, the charity is been dedicated to supporting boys and men at key transitional moments in their lives. They support young men engaged in their programme to develop positive, functional and rewarding ways of being men. It's driven by the core belief that by providing young men with the tools and confidence to discover what positive, functional and rewarding forms of masculinity look like, a better future is possible. One which creates happier, healthier futures for boys, men and everyone who is a part of their world.

After hearing Owen interviewed on a podcast called 'Now and men',[3] where he spoke about being invited to the G7 summit in Cornwall to speak to the Duchess of Cambridge and Jill Biden about the charity's work with fathers, I was intrigued by their approach. Owen's words kept me company on the long drive home from a frustratingly unproductive meeting at a school about their 'problematic young men' in the North of England. More importantly, they also left me feeling hopeful. Having been engaged in their work since the year I was born, Future Men had a wealth of experience I could only dream of. Striking a fatherly figure, Owen spoke with a gentle eloquence about his journey with the organisation. I was immediately taken by his reflections on Future Men's strengths-based approach and the local nature of their work.

Speaking with an East London twang which evidenced his lifelong connection to the area as a young man, father and later grandfather, Owen emphasised the importance of Future Men's situatedness within working-class communities. He, and the organisation he worked for, prided themselves on the depth of knowledge and understanding they had about where their young men were from. Whether it was aligned to their work chairing the All-Party Parliamentary Group on Fatherhood,[4] or their activities with young men in educational settings through the Boys Development Programme,[5] Future Men embraced the role that social history played in their day-to-day interactions. They embedded the work within the lives and communities of those they sought to support.

For Owen, the localised nature of Future Men's activity was important. It provided a direct connection to the young men's lives and experiences. Just as growing up in a small, predominately White, West Midlands town fundamentally shaped my friendships, interests and opinions as a young man, Owen's experiences as a young working-class Black man growing up in London did the same. It created connection and understanding. Future Men were not some middle-class 'missionaries' coming to save the young working-class men of London from themselves – quite the opposite. Owen had been there. He got it, he had lived it and he cared.

Rather than shying away from the fact that the young men's experiences were embedded within a societal structure that put them in a position of power and comparative privilege in their relationships with women, Owen was keen to locate the work of the charity within it. He talked at length about wider

gender-based inequalities and the charity's role in addressing
them. He argued that rather than the young men he worked
with being disinclined to pursue greater involvement in family
life and parenting, often the opposite was true. However, within
such an endeavour, there were significant challenges facing young
working-class fathers. Their access to secure, well-paying jobs,
their levels of education and access to services which supported
good physical and mental health all made the process more
difficult. It resonated with a lot of research being conducted
in regions outside of London by projects such as Following
Young Fathers Further,[6] exploring how class, masculinity and
inequality intersected to create barriers for young working-class
men's parental involvement. Throughout our conversation,
Owen went to great lengths to highlight the important role
that social structures and systems that encompassed the lives
of the young men played when articulating their experiences.
Contrary to narratives which seek to individualise the challenges
they experienced, he believed that it was only through a deep
understanding of the active role that these played in their lives
that meaningful change could be achieved:

> It's all based in patriarchy. Our policies and our
> systems are not keeping up with what modern men
> and women want, which is a more equitable and
> equal distribution of domestic labour. More equitable
> access to the marketplace and to the workplace for
> men and women. So that we don't have to fit into
> the traditional models and be fairer with each other
> about what we do. Have a more equal distribution
> across the board of this stuff and try to close the gaps
> that do exist.

As seen with the Piers Morgan interview, there has been a
collective aversion to recognising the legacy of socio-economic
inequality for young people in London, and Owen's reflections
point directly to its consequences. The idea of a disconnect
between the desires, interests and orientations of working-class
young men, and the ability of societal systems and structures to
meet them, featured as strongly within his commentary as they

did in research with working-class young men in Wales or the North of England. While it could be argued that the social history of the area was different from those deindustrialised towns and cities, their position as young working-class men still restricted what they deemed to be possible. Whether it was a willingness to step back into the workplace, or a desire to take up greater responsibility in domestic and family life, the political, social and economic machinery which governed such opportunities in London gave them little room to do so.

Of course, Owen was speaking with specific regard to family rather than education and work; however, he also pointed to the fact that there may be differences. That a collective experience of navigating social and economic change in different places and contexts will of course create different histories. Collective memories which shape recollections, dispositions and experiences. The perception of opportunities and a tacit knowledge of how to take them. During my time with Owen, I was keen to get his take on what those differences were and how they influenced the future opportunities of working-class young men in London:

> It's about the pace of movement. We know that the country is tilting economically to the South East. You know, soon Scotland will be up in the air and London will go underwater! It's just as a graphic representation of how resources are distributed around the country. How people gravitate toward London and the South East because of opportunity. Basically, for me it's borne out of London and Britain deindustrialising. But the opportunities for new industries and new ways of earning, the creative industries and service industries tend to have been more live and more plentiful in London.

He reflected that where he sat in Bermondsey, home of Millwall football club, was a historically working-class area of the city, populated by communities who used to make their living working on the docks of the River Thames. But with deindustrialisation and globalisation came the disintegration of opportunities for jobs in traditionally working-class professions. While in many areas of the country there was little opportunity to fill the employment gap with other work, London was different. With better transport links in the city came greater opportunity for mobility to find work in other parts of the city. After the passing of Thatcher's Housing Act in 1980, he also described how working-class people's ability to buy their council houses, followed by the rapid inflation of property prices, meant that they were put at a relative economic advantage. With demand for London-based properties booming, many working-class men established new ways of working. Hopping on the train or the bus, they found jobs in the trades, servicing the increased demand with employment as builders, plumbers and electricians:

> Ultimately, I think some of the economic shifts are very much the same as in other parts of the country, but in London we've had an accelerated process in the transition from an industrial to a post-industrial society. With being more advanced, more working-class people can take advantage. But there's still a massive disparity. In fact, over the last 20 years particularly, I would say the gaps have got wider. That little moment of opportunity under Margaret Thatcher where working-class people had a chance; that shift in capital from the state into the hands of private ownership, which gave a boost, it's gone. That opportunity doesn't exist anymore. If you weren't one of those families who were lucky enough to be able to do that at that time and you still live here, you're even further away now than you ever were. Further away from getting on the property market or having a job that earns enough to sustain you living in central inner-city London.

There were still a significant number of working-class families who, for whatever reason, weren't well positioned to take advantage of this rare opportunity to secure a foothold on the housing ladder or secure 'good' jobs in the trades. Owen explained that while opportunities to work in the service sector or the gig economy are more plentiful in London than in other areas, pay is low. As a result, the gaps in wages and wealth are as wide as ever:

> The service sector is one that's difficult for some men to engage with because it feels as though it doesn't fit into their ideas of the kind of man they want to be, or the kind of jobs they want to do now. Necessity is the mother of invention, and people take what they can get. But I know from the work that we do with some people that rather than, you know, be a one-star server at McDonald's working by the end of a till and getting food for people, people will choose other means of making money. Ways that boost their self-esteem, give them morale or give them more status where they live, rather than fitting into some of those industries. And if education doesn't give them a pathway or their familial relationships don't give them a pathway into a family business where they can be a good earner which competes with the money I can make through other means, they'll find other ways.

Alongside the issues related to pay, Owen emphasises the importance placed on the perception of such work, which makes it an unappealing prospect. Although employment opportunities in fast food restaurants, shops and bars may be more readily available in London than in other areas of England, they also carry with them low status. In a situation where, in much the same way as other geographic areas with an industrial heritage, familial networks and educational outcomes haven't provided a route in to work that holds financial or social rewards, the young men he works with often seek an alternative means to make up the shortfall.

As the chief executive officer of a charity, Owen hadn't had the opportunity to read much of the more recent research mentioned in the last chapter on masculinity, class and transitions into work for young working-class men. However, the parallels within his take on London's recent socio-economic history are clear. Deindustrialisation, and the accompanying shift to a service-driven economy, had a significant impact on London's working-class communities. But in his view there were key differences which set London apart. Transport infrastructure across the city was more robust, meaning more accessible options for work. Faster-paced growth in the creative industries and the service sector meant there was a greater range of options for employment. In London, these opportunities arrived faster and were more accessible to working-class men than in other areas. The chance for residents to buy their council houses, followed by rapid inflation in house prices, significantly increased the relative wealth of individuals who were positioned to take advantage of the opportunity to become homeowners. In his account, he describes how these amalgamated to offer an element of protection that may not have existed in other areas of the country such as cities in the North of England.

But, as Owen reflects, London's specific socio-economic conditions also brought challenges. While house price inflation benefitted the previous generation of homeowners, the rapid increase in house prices made getting a foot on the property ladder nearly impossible for those who weren't able to buy their council houses. The rise of employment opportunities linked with the service economy was coupled with an increase in low-paid, precarious jobs. While work in the creative economy had also boomed, often opportunities were restricted to individuals who could afford to undertake the significant amount of unpaid work which was often required to 'get a foot in the door'.[7]

In much the same way as Akala had done in his Good Morning Britain discussion on serious youth violence, Owen deconstructed the elements which contribute to the challenges that some of the young men who engage with the charity face:

> The geographic and psychological boundaries for young men from particular areas of London are shrinking. Because of youth violence and other factors, because of the growth of certain cultures around territorialism. Even though they live in London, the spaces that young men occupy are becoming smaller and smaller as the years go by, unfortunately; particularly if they're caught up in some of the challenging issues of group association and territorial spaces.

While London may be a sprawling metropolis with a well-serviced infrastructure, this often fails to neatly transpose into freedom of movement for young working-class men. There are serious social challenges for those who occupy these spaces to navigate, and they're fraught with risk. Territorialism and serious youth violence, the features of which are powerfully described in Akala's book *Natives*, mean geographic borders and spaces in which the young men feel safe and secure are tightly bound. While London is an enormous city, it becomes significantly smaller if a violent encounter could be waiting for you at the next tube station.

Alongside this, as described by Reni Eddo-Lodge in her bestselling book *Why I'm No Longer Talking to White People about Race*,[8] there is a deep, and justified, mistrust of law enforcement among Black Londoners. Experiences of racial profiling and tragedies such as the murder of Stephen Lawrence and the subsequent MacPherson Inquiry branding the Metropolitan Police 'institutionally racist' have resulted in intergenerational mistrust. More recently, in an incident reported by BBC News in 2023,[9] two Metropolitan Police officers were sacked for gross misconduct after being found guilty of racial profiling, having lied about smelling cannabis as an excuse to stop and search professional athletes Bianca Williams and Ricardo Dos Santos. The article later quotes Steven Noonan from the Independent Office for Police Conduct, who states: 'We know that black people are almost nine times more likely to be stopped and searched by police than white people, and nearly nine times more likely to be searched for drugs, despite a lower "find rate" of drugs for black people than white people.'

While it might be the case that young men in predominately White working-class communities don't often experience favourable profiling by the police, there is little sign of the levels of acute targeting, and at times harassment, experienced by their Black counterparts in London. Owen reflects that when the agencies established for protection and service are perceived as being just as likely to harm as to help, there is little option but to look after yourself:

> There are risks inherent to boys and men around some of the traditional masculinities that they're conditioned to value and can be practically useful to them in the areas that they live in. For example, not showing weakness, being strong, and solving issues or

defending yourself with violence are all common. The result of not having all these safety nets around you means that your threshold and your resilience; when things go wrong or when you're challenged, may be a lot lower than other people. You're quicker to react in what would be deemed an aggressive way.

When faced with such conditions, he spoke to the utilitarian value of masculine practices which offer an element of protection. Not showing weakness by displaying certain emotions, being strong and being ready to resolve issues through violence all have a certain practical value in a setting where the risk of being subject to an attack is high. However, without the safety that comes with financial security – a home, enough money to pay the bills, enough food – young working-class men are placed in a precarious position. Anxieties about not having these things are an ever-present companion. It's a feeling that affects you physically, mentally and emotionally. A gnawing static at the back of your head, an ever-present anxiety that comes with the knowledge that you're one piece of bad luck away from destitution. When Owen talks of resilience, he's talking about the implications of this constant buzz, one which becomes louder in situations of heightened emotional intensity. Where, against a backdrop of masculine expectation, the pressure to solve issues with violence is interwoven with your worth and value, you are fast to react aggressively to threat.

The pressures are competing, conflicting and, he reflects, often place young men at a crossroads. A junction in which where there is no safe route out of a situation. Undesirable consequences accompany any choice, and decisions simply become an exercise in limiting their severity. During our discussion, Owen used the example of a teenage boy at school who experienced pressure to engage in sexist and homophobic behaviour. He asserts that at a time when young men's sense of self is not set, a time of vulnerability, they may gravitate toward what they perceive as a 'safe' model of masculine behaviour. For many, this model is 'uber masculine'. In a high stakes game of social survival, uber masculinity offers the best protection. If young men don't conform, they make themselves vulnerable to becoming a target. It boils down to a choice – you're either with us or against us:

> There are risks of not conforming to those tropes and those stereotypes on an immediate day-to-day basis. If I'm at school and I'm 14, and I'm saying look I don't want to say bad things about the women in my area. I don't want to be involved in a homophobic japery about someone in class who doesn't conform with me it can be dangerous. You risk becoming the butt of all of those jokes. If you're not with us, you're against us.

Owen explains that when young men are placed under acute pressure to conform, there is only a limited space to engage in reflection on the longer-term risks inherent in such behaviours. While at school this might be limited to joining in with 'banter', it can also be the start of a journey, one which, later down the line, gradually evolves into committing violent acts or engaging in criminal activity. In subverting normative masculine expectations, in not being 'man enough', not 'being real', there is an immediate risk of harm and social exclusion. However, each time a young man succumbs to the pressure, they distance themselves from the mechanisms by which a future characterised by happy, healthy relationships can be realised. Whether it be sanctioning by teachers at school and marginalisation in education, perpetrating violent acts or getting arrested and entering into the criminal justice system, they are all have the same root cause. – economic inequality, masculinity and the expectations associated with being a young working-class man in London.

Rather than the stereotypical narratives which paint young men as naturally anti-authoritarian and aggressive 'lads', Owen frames such behaviour as inherently linked to the risks and opportunities afforded by their social, economic and geographic location. In much the same way as Ward's Wales-based research in the previous chapter, he describes the young men as positioning themselves in a continual unspoken dialogue with masculine expectations which are inscribed into the structures of their social world:

> The key is real problem solving. Giving young men the skills to critically think for themselves and analyse

their circumstances. To see how some of the models they've been given don't work well for them. That has to be married hand in hand with practical solutions to their everyday environment.

Shining a light on those longer-term, less immediate risks, and equipping young working-class men with the tools to think practically and critically about how their actions may contribute to them, has been Owen's life's work. His charity encourages young men to examine the models of masculinity provided to them in relation to their own lived experience. In a non-judgemental, supportive manner, they are provided with the tools to decide for themselves what the consequences of certain choices and life trajectories may be. While Future Men conduct some amazing activity, they do so within strict limitations. Owen reflects that for the work to be truly successful, a change is required within wider society. A means for the work to be married with practical, material support. Mechanisms which lessen the background hum of anxious static resulting from inadequate housing, high bills and financial insecurity. A change that Future Men are not able to realise on their own.

From the conversation with Owen, it is very apparent that the experiences of the individuals Future Men engage with are very different from the young men in Burntwood, Newcastle or Swansea. The course of socio-economic change played out very differently in London than in other areas of England. London is also a place which has significantly more ethnic diversity. A range of cultural heritages and socio-historical experiences which make up a city with a population size nearly double that of Scotland. Through the writing of critical thinkers such as Akala, and others such as Eddo-Lodge, Jason Arday[10] and Derron Wallace,[11] we can see how the intersections of race and cultural heritage sharpen the edges of inequality. How societal structures which are still bound within systems borne out of a colonial past perpetuate compounded experiences of inequality for people of colour. As I mentioned at the top of the chapter, navigating those particular sharp edges is not something I can speak about with any real degree of understanding or authenticity, so instead I implore you to listen to the words of those who do.

However, there are also elements of those journeys into manhood which bring young men of different ethnicities, from different towns and cities, together under an umbrella of shared experience. When we look at what characterises the 'uber masculine' behaviours described by Owen, they really don't look so different from those which were discussed in previous chapters by young White, working-class men outside of London. As Akala so eloquently described in the Piers Morgan interview, that is because they are caused by the same foundational issue: material inequality. For those studying social histories, the intergenerational journeys of young working-class men in London might look very different from those of young working-class men in Burntwood, and they are. But what becomes apparent through their reflections is that those differences have been used to camouflage a fundamental shared truth. A knowledge which holds equal weight for young working-class men regardless of where they live in the UK. Whether it be Bermondsey or Burntwood, it is the same material inequality that perpetuates, entrenches and limits the potential for young men to escape the tight bonds placed around them. When mixed with 'taken-for-granted' assumptions about what constitutes manhood, the chances of marginalisation in education, mental ill health, violence and entry into the criminal justice system increase. In lives characterised by precarity and risk, compliance with masculine expectation is rewarded with an instantaneous hit of acceptance and belonging. Wherever it is that these men may live, deviation from these expectations is not worth the price that will be paid as a result.

6

Making the grades: teachers, schools and masculine expectations

My mum recently said that getting kicked out of school was the best thing that could have happened to me. It was a strange thing to bring up over Sunday dinner, but educationally, she was probably right.

Following my exclusion, the hunt began for a new place to study. Due to various feuds with other young men from the local area, it was decided a move to the other school in my hometown wouldn't end well. My expulsion had stirred up a bit of angst among the lads I associated with at the time. Things were tense. Whether or not I had said whom I had bought the cannabis from during the interrogation leading to my expulsion became a subject of much debate and contestation. Incidentally, I hadn't grassed. I was fully aware of what the consequences of doing so would mean. I wasn't stupid enough. Despite unrelenting pressure from the school's headteacher, my parents and a local police officer, my mouth remained firmly shut. However, at the time, the young men in my hometown only had my word for it. For some, it wasn't good enough.

In hindsight, I'm very pleased that this portion of my life took place in a small town. As discussed in the previous chapter, in a larger city the risks would have been far higher. Had that been the case, things may have escalated into much more serious violence. But still, the notion that I'd grassed about who was selling drugs locally, even if it wasn't true, placed me uncomfortably under the spotlight. While I was out and about, there were numerous young men whom it would have been very bad for me to have bumped into. For the next couple of years, leaving the house became entwined with risk to my personal safety. Increased heart rate, fists clenched into balls in my pockets. Constantly looking over my shoulder and anticipating who would be around the next corner. It was exhausting.

What made it worse was that it was based in fact. My earlier struggles with anxiety had been a projection of risk and worry on to situations that didn't warrant a fight-or-flight response. This situation most certainly did. Being chased when I was spotted out at a local park by the wrong group of lads and having to hide in a friend's house for hours. Being unlucky with my timing on the bus home and having the misfortune to bump into a couple of lads who, clubs in hand, had just finished a game of golf at the local pitch and putt.

As such, it was decided that another school near my hometown wasn't a good idea. Instead, the search was widened. After a brief stint at home making good use of the bedroom fortress, I started at a new school in a town about 6 miles away several months later.

Although getting there only took half an hour by bus, it may as well have been on another planet.

My new school first opened its doors in 1495. Prior to its merger with a secondary modern in 1971, the institution had been a selective grammar school for nearly 500 years. Notable alumni included the scholar and compiler of an English dictionary Dr Samuel Johnson,[1] actor David Garrick[2] and essayist Joseph Addison.[3] Although it had not been a grammar school for nearly 40 years prior to my arrival, the school had a reputation which matched its history. While just 18 per cent of young people from my home postcode went to university, the progression rate of young people residing in the postcode of my second school stood at around 65 per cent.[4] I'm still a little bit flummoxed as to why they let me in.

Although it's always difficult to draw concrete conclusions from data like these, it would appear that by getting myself excluded from school I had moved to another one in a postcode where, compared with my hometown, students were over three times more likely to progress to university. My previous experience of school did very little to prepare me for this new educational playing field. Once again, I was entered into a game and expected to participate without quite knowing the rules. The basics were all the same: uniform, lessons, teachers and football at lunchtime, but that's where the similarities ended.

Rather than the jumper and polo shirt I was used to, uniform was a shirt, tie and blazer, a blazer which you weren't allowed to take off unless you received special permission because it was hot. Even this had its own name, a 'shirt sleeve order'. Each day coming home from school I would cover the distance between the bus stop and my house at record-breaking speed, hoping no one from my area would spot me in the ridiculous outfit I had to wear.

While adapting to the new school rules and the poncy uniform was annoying, it paled in comparison to the most significant and pressing challenge I faced – figuring out how to fit in.

On my first day, two students from my new tutor group volunteered to show me around. Once out of earshot of the teachers, I asked them the question I was sure would facilitate fast track ingratiation into the social hierarchy, 'where can I go for a cigarette and not get caught?' They looked at me like I was wearing dead cats as slippers.

From then on, I realised that things were going to be very different. That's not to say that there weren't a group of students at the school who smoked, there were, but they also weren't particularly popular. Nor were the boys who proactively disrupted lessons, or explicitly contested the authority of the teachers. No one seemed to become a target for engaging with their learning. Some of the most popular students were also in top sets for lessons. When they did argue with a teacher, it was in an effort to outsmart them, using their perceived intellectual superiority as a means to undermine the teacher's authority. Even when they were acting rebelliously, they were practising skills and gaining experience that aligned with a trajectory into middle-class education and employment.

Rather than people's parents working in trades or the service industry, they were doctors and solicitors. Hardly anyone spoke about the job they were going to get straight after school; instead, discussions took place around A level selections and university choices. Of course, the local college was always an option, but it was the undesirable consequence of educational failure. A 'less good' avenue which was treated with a level of disdain.

Success was good GCSEs, strong A levels and a place at a Russell Group university.

Bullying still took place, but it was more covert, sneakier. Rather than getting beaten up, victims were far more likely to be targeted for assault psychologically. I shudder at the recollections of vile, hateful comments whispered in lessons to some of my classmates who were overweight or disabled. It was cruel and vindictive. Torment was physical too, but you were more likely to get locked in a cupboard than punched in the face. Although fights did happen occasionally, they were far rarer.

Essentially, the tools I had developed to survive at my first school were now next to useless. In this new blazer-wearing, university-going, insult-whispering educational arena, the rules were different. A tug of war began to take place between who and what I was expected to be. I was still living in the same place, but each morning I jumped on the bus and was transported to an alternate social reality.

Adapting to this new environment took a considerable amount of work. I became hyper aware of everything I said and did. While experiences at my first school were problematic in many ways, the rules with masculinity and behaviour in the classroom were clear and simple. Here, they were nuanced and complex. Each misstep resulted in numerous forms of social sanction. It was like being a football fan who'd turned up to the ground on the wrong day and accidentally found himself at a rugby match. Same stadium, same seat, but a very different game.

Again, my willingness to get into physical altercations afforded me a level of protection, but by the end of my first year I was firmly established on the social peripheries. The teachers were very different too. United in their perception of me as a troublemaker, I was treated by many with varying degrees of hostility. They were almost systematic in their communication of how little they expected from my academic performance and future educational prospects.

On a recent visit home, my parents handed me a pile of old school reports they had found in the loft. As I was leafing through the one from year 11, I read a particularly poignant piece of career forecasting from my head of year: 'Alex will never be a rocket scientist, and probably not a doctor or a lawyer. But he has matured into a pleasant, polite and charming young man.' Given the fact that I got a PhD in 2020, I do hope that this teacher never left her role as an educator to begin a full-time career in fortune telling. However, she was also one of the few staff members who, in hindsight, was probably trying really hard to do her best by me. Determined to keep a hawk-like eye on my progress, for two years my parents received weekly letters from her about where on the premises I was taking up residence to have a ciggy at breaktime, her suspicions about what those cigarettes 'contained' and other theories about 'nefarious activities' I was engaged with.

She was largely wrong about everything other than the fact I was having a cigarette. Often going by myself, these snatched 15 minutes of solitude were a release from the social pressure cooker. Ironically, it was one of the few times of the day where I felt I could breathe.

Over time, I gradually learned the unwritten rules of the new school classroom. How I could use my intelligence to annoy teachers who were more explicit in their expressions of disdain for my character without getting into trouble. I began to adopt a verbal communication style that could be antagonistic but 'appropriate' for the classroom. And I was good at it. I thrived in lessons where I was allowed to engage in discussion and debate. Where I was allowed to have an opinion. I hated lessons that involved learning facts, formulas and rules to regurgitate in an exam but loved those in which I could critique, create and discuss. The desire in me to prove people wrong became burning. To show the staff that I was 'good enough' to be there. To frustrate their prejudice by getting good exam results and going to university.

One of the key differences between here and my first school was that the social sanctions for open displays of engagement in learning were not nearly as apparent. At my new school, I didn't have to worry about the risk of physical or psychological injury because of putting my hand up and getting a question right. Students engaged in extracurricular activities like music, drama and debate while maintaining their popularity. In this regard, I had a newfound freedom. There were very few links between my friends at home and my classmates at school. They would never find out. I was safe to enjoy learning.

So, I scraped the required GCSEs for entry to sixth form (and was extremely pleased by the looks on some of the teacher's faces when they realised they'd have to put up with me for another two years). For the first time, school was a place I didn't mind going to. I still suffered the consequences of low expectations from teachers – the predicted grades that populated my UCAS application were woeful – but I was studying subjects I enjoyed, and I loved it.

I achieved two to three grades higher in my A-level exams than the teacher's predictions in each subject, but by that time it was too late. Of the five universities I applied to, I was rejected outright by three. However, the University of Wolverhampton offered me a place on a drama degree, and I began life as a student in 2007.

It's ironic that my future educational orientations developed not out of lofty ambitions to 'reach for the stars' or buying into a narrative that peddled the 'gold standard' of a future trajectory in education and work which involved moving away from home to study at a Russell Group university. Instead, it was a deep love for learning. A passion for education, alongside an intrinsic motivation to prove educators wrong who, given my background and circumstances, should have been a source of encouragement and support. Instead, many played the opposite role. Had I listened to the judgements they had made about my educational aptitude, worth and value, I would most certainly not be writing this book.

Unfortunately, young men from working-class backgrounds facing similar challenges in education is not at all uncommon. In fact, it plays out all too frequently. It is evident in both their educational attainment and the rates of progression to university. Department for Education data tell us that of all White British young men who are eligible for free school meals, just 13 per cent enter into higher education.[5] This compares with 37 per cent of those who are not eligible. For young men of White and Black Caribbean heritage, the figures are equally dim, standing at 18 per cent and 34 per cent respectively. The gap is stark and intrinsically linked to GCSE results. Prior to the pandemic, the proportion of working-class young men achieving a grade nine to five in GCSE maths and english in my home county was a little under 15 per cent. For those from more affluent backgrounds, the percentage doubled.

So, what is going on in education that's causing young men from working-class backgrounds to be less than half as likely to pass their GCSEs or go to university as their middle-class male counterparts? While we have already discussed numerous reasons which play out beyond the school gate in previous chapters, what happens in the school classroom plays a significant part too. And I can think of no better person to introduce some of the challenges than Mark Roberts.

Mark

I first became aware of Mark's work when I was asked to review a copy of a book he had written with a colleague called *Boys Don't Try: Rethinking Masculinity in Schools*.[6] While the book is very much a synthesis of existing thought and research in education, it provides a skilful summation of the numerous challenges facing young working-class men in the classroom. The book is an accessible way to understand a variety of elements which intersect to mean that the outcomes of young working-class men have become one of the most wicked challenges facing the UK educational system. It provides a whistlestop tour of how issues like inequality, relationships, violence, peer pressure and pornography culminate in harmful behaviour and disproportionately low exam results for young men.

After finishing the book, I found Mark's details online and reached out, and we set up our first meeting back in 2020. Since then, we've stayed in touch and shared a platform at numerous conferences and events. What I love about Mark is his authenticity. Although now residing in Northern Ireland, Mark's strong Yorkshire accent shines through with every syllable he utters. Appearing on my screen wearing a shirt and tie with rolled-up sleeves after finishing teaching an English lesson, he immediately came across to me as someone who 'got it'. At the time, I would have been hard pressed to articulate exactly what 'getting it' meant, but it was clear to me that he did. Now, after a few more years of research and work in the area of masculinity and educational inequality under my belt, I can describe 'it' with a little more eloquence. What Mark, like many of the other contributors interviewed for this book possessed, was a deep understanding which seemed to permeate his being. He was not talking about the educational challenges faced by young working-class men in the abstract but rather with a depth of comprehension that can only come from lived experience. While technological advancements in educational systems and structures surrounding the young men made their experiences different from his own, having to navigate them as a young working-class man gave Mark a strong sense of connection to those he wrote about and worked alongside.

Since 2021, Mark has spoken to thousands of educators, spreading his message far and wide across the teaching profession. As well as writing a second book, *The Boy Question: How to Teach Boys to Succeed in School*,[7] he has continued to work as a full-time teacher, putting the principles he talks about into practice with young men on a daily basis.

Though he is now one of the UK's leading voices in debates surrounding young men in education, this is certainly not what Mark thought he'd spend his professional life doing at the age of 14. Similar to myself, his trajectory through compulsory education was a turbulent one. Growing up in an ex-mining town in West Yorkshire, he describes his own experience in secondary education as 'disastrous'. In a concerted effort to hide his intelligence, Mark spent most of his time at school 'deliberately pretending to be less intelligent than I was, so I didn't get lumped in with the geeks and the swots'. He quickly cottoned on to the risks associated with standing out from the crowd. In a school with a culture of violence, where life was 'dog eat dog', his natural size and athleticism afforded him a measure of protection. However, he was acutely aware that if he 'worked too hard and was too keen in lessons, that could change'.

Coming from a community where ideas of masculinity were strongly linked to work in the trades and using your hands, Mark described how his uncle saw his interest in education and learning as 'a bit suspect'. It misaligned with his views on what 'real men' should and shouldn't do. As an intelligent young man, he found himself walking a tightrope between a yearning to be popular and socially included and a hidden desire to learn and do well academically. In our conversation, he reflected that he spent his time in the classroom knowing most of the answers to questions and wanting to answer them but never quite allowing himself to do it:

> Yeah, I was very, very lucky not to be permanently excluded. I think that the only reason that they didn't permanently exclude me, is that I basically didn't really go for the last year or two. They knew that I was going to do enough to get reasonable grades, so they kind of left me alone. They didn't follow up on my truancy that much, otherwise I think I would have been permanently excluded as well. I was very fortunate not to. I think for me, that the self-sabotage was very much tied into risk-taking behaviour.
>
> So you know, I'd frequently go to school, go to exams drunk and things like that, and would do outrageous things to try to impress my mates. It was often that even they'd be shocked by how outrageous some of the things that I would do were. I think that risk taking for me was a form of kind of self-harm. I suppose a lot of it was tied into really struggling to navigate these two halves of my personality where I secretly wanted to do really well but also tried to fit in. Risk is something that very much comes out.

This internal struggle between the competing desires of acceptance and respect from his peers and his desire to learn placed Mark under an incredible amount of pressure. The self-sabotaging behaviours he engaged in slowly became riskier and more outrageous. Looking back, he views the behaviour of his younger self as a form of self-harm. When few alternatives were available, it was a way he could exercise what little agency his position as a working-class boy at school afforded him. The shocking things he did provided a degree of status and protection within his masculine peer group, but they had consequences for him psychologically, emotionally and educationally.

As a teenager, at a time when the pressures associated with navigating this tension were most acute, Mark left school. His exam results meant that he could have continued to study A levels, but he chose not to. In the long-running battle between what he wanted to do and what he felt he should do, conforming to what was expected of him won out. He followed a trajectory into work which cemented his identity as a working-class lad in a working-class community. Leaving school at the first available opportunity, he picked up a job in a factory making industrial gearboxes shortly after his GCSE exams:

> I think a few teachers picked me up on it. A few teachers found me out. They could see behind this kind of idiotic façade. They would say, you know, you could really go places, you could really go to top universities and things like that. But the pull of peer pressure was just far, far too strong for me. I left school at 16 with on paper, decent GCSEs, but nowhere near what they should have been.

It wasn't until nearly five years later, at the age of 20, that his desire to learn won out, and Mark returned to education. However, doing so later in life again put him under significant pressure:

> I got there, but it was a very, very hard route. It cost me a lot to get to that stage. You know, lots of family problems. My parents had really had enough of me. So, I suppose linking that back to my interest in this area, I wanted to work out why boys like me were doing what they were doing. And not just boys like me who, you know, people had said are really smart, who can go on and do things like this. But why boys in general? Why was there this attitude in my school that it was embarrassing to work hard? That it was really uncool to do homework and to want to do well. It was unusual to have these expectations that you'd go on and do well. Why was it something that was absolutely not considered? I really wanted to understand what was going on here. I suppose it's what led me on a very long road which ended eventually in teaching.

Although bucking the expectations of family members and friends was difficult, Mark's desire to critically understand the role masculinity and social class played during his own time in the classroom won out. Igniting a drive and determination to put his education to purpose, he went to university, trained as a teacher and began working at an inner-city all-boys comprehensive school in Manchester.

Mark describes the institution as a tough place where, much like his own school, it was 'survival of the fittest'. As a result, he leant on some of the ways of being a man that worked for him as a student. He fell into the trap of trying to prove himself. Justifying his presence by being laddish and leaning into stereotypical masculine interests such as rugby and football to affirm his status with the students. As you'd expect, his way of being was enmeshed within a reflection of his own experiences in education as a young man. The interests, attitudes and behaviours he relied on as a student were now finding their way into his practice as a teacher. He 'taught to stereotypes'.

It was only after a significant period, and a lot of wider research and reading, that Mark was able to reflect on the consequences of this stereotypical approach for his teaching practice. And he didn't like what he saw. A critical examination of how he was doing things and why led him to feel like he was actively contributing to the problem rather than the solution:

> So very much as a teacher to begin with I thought 'OK well boys don't seem to enjoy doing some of the things that I'm trying to teach them, so let's do it differently. Let's use these engagement strategies like sport as a kind of hook. Let's bring in things like competition, try to make things more practical, hands on; limit the amount of writing and reading'. I involved use of technology as a bit of a bribe. You know, 'sorry, we're gonna have to do a bit of writing, but we'll get the iPads out later on if you focus for 20 minutes'. All of that kind of stuff is really indicative of lower expectations for boys. In my own practice, that was probably the biggest turning point. Realising that all of the things that I thought I was doing to help, were actually hindering.

I think that the teacher's expectations of boys are absolutely foundational to any understanding of this; not just the gender attainment gaps, but everything else that goes with it. There's a whole body of research that shows that, when it comes to academic potential, behaviour and the way that things are assessed, teachers have lower expectations of boys.

Going through this process brought Mark to an uncomfortable revelation. The evidence suggested that the seismic gap in educational attainment for young working-class men had as much to do with the teachers as it did the students. In much the same way as in the discussion surrounding aspiration earlier on in the book, Mark had uncovered one of the most damaging assumptions surrounding the education of working-class boys in schools: that the fault, responsibility and onus for change lay entirely with the young men themselves.

Mark has now written about this extensively. Engaging with research conducted by academics such as Susan Jones, Debra Myhill[8] and Carolyn Jackson,[9] he began to approach the problem from a different angle. Critically exploring the contribution of learning, teaching and school culture, he began to understand the instrumental role that teachers' attitudes and expectations played in the education of young working-class men:

It's hard to escape the feeling that there is this systemic bias against boys … Because boys may come across like I was, as frustrating to teach at times and self-sabotaging at times, teachers struggle to see beyond that. As a result, they assume that boys are weak compared to girls. So, I think that teacher expectations are absolutely massive. Some of the classic studies that I talk about all the time are ones like the Myhill and Jones study, 2004,[10] where they look at troublesome boys and compliant girls.

But then you can also look at the stuff around assessment and marking. The way that you've got these clear biases against boys as well. I think teacher expectations are something that if we're going to deal with these issues, it's the number one thing that we probably need to tackle in the classroom and in schools.

In articulating these thoughts, Mark is acutely aware that he is placing his head above the educational parapet. It's an uncomfortable realisation, and one which is not accepted readily. For teachers, the idea that the burden of responsibility for educational 'success' doesn't lie entirely on the shoulders of the young men they teach can be uncomfortable, even jarring.

Despite its grounding in research and evidence, the idea that our classroom cultures, and the underlying stereotypes and assumptions which underpin them, are even partially responsible is difficult to accept. Being told that it's time to hold a mirror up to all those comfortable, familiar assumptions we hold about young men in the classroom and question them is not an easy thing to do. The sense of safety and familiarity in trusting what you 'know' about the young men in front of you disappears. Your mantle of expert is removed. Instead, you are placed in the precarious position of needing to learn from those who had previously been neatly placed in a box labelled 'difficult' and 'troublesome'.

In doing so, teachers are asked to lift a portion of responsibility for 'problematic behaviour' from the shoulders of the young man and attach it to themselves. To their practice as educators and school leaders. It leaves people feeling uncertain, vulnerable and at risk. When being asked to reflect so deeply and so critically, I have seen it invoke defensiveness and even anger from staff. Although sad, this is completely understandable. Schools and teachers dedicate their lives to providing the young people in their care with the tools they need to have the best possible exam results and future opportunities. Being told that, as Mark suggests, they may unwittingly be damaging the educational outcomes of the very same young people that they commit their lives to supporting can be jarring.

However, in highlighting research which shows that young men are disproportionately labelled as 'class clowns' or 'troublemakers' from a young age, and talking about the harm such stereotypes cause to the educational attainment, future prospects and happiness of young men,[11] Mark is not pointing a finger at individuals who work in schools. Instead, he is highlighting the undesirable consequence of a culture that permeates our education system and wider society. A mainstream, unconscious, taken-for-granted assumption which means such labels are embraced, adopted and attached to young men, both inside and outside the classroom, from an incredibly early age.

The conversation I had with Mark was wide ranging. He spoke about how such assumptions played out in teaching and learning, behaviour and sanctioning, mentoring, negotiations of masculinity and the use of male role models. He acknowledged the limitations of an educator's contact with a student in terms of time, and the wider things going on in young men's lives which a teacher may have little power to control. However, while the examples given were specific and numerous, they coalesced around a theme which held true for teachers and students alike:

> I can't control how much homework they do. I can't control what time they go to sleep on a night or how many hours they play on the Xbox, or the messages they get from parents about the importance of homework. I can't control any of that, but I can have a massive influence on the way that I communicate to them in my classroom about my expectations. I can control the language that I use and my tone when I talk to them. I need to listen.

In the earlier interview with Mike Nicholson from Progressive Masculinity, Mike had outlined the need to equip young men from working-class backgrounds with the tools and understanding to engage critically with the role of masculinity in their own lives. For Mark, critical engagement by educators with their role in the lives of young men is of vital importance. And evidence suggests that the demonstration of care that would accompany such a move can have a powerful impact.

In recent research conducted by the Taking Boys Seriously team in Northern Ireland with 442 adolescent boys aged 12–18,[12] respondents spoke highly of educators who:

• understood their point of view;
• appreciated the issues they may face outside of school;

- connected with boys and listened to their point of view;
- challenged them, but in a supportive way.

In other words, they valued the feeling of being listened to and understood. They respected educators who appreciated the complex negotiations taking place within their own lives, who held high expectations for them and challenged the young men to meet them. Of the respondents, 85 per cent agreed that they were more likely to learn when they knew their voice and views were valued in an educational context. In accompanying focus groups and interviews, researchers highlighted that 'boys spoke of rarely being given opportunities to discuss masculine norms and social pressures such as identity formation, sectarianism, and experiences of male violence'.[13]

While it is important to acknowledge that the social and political landscape of Northern Ireland is very different from that which Mark speaks about in England, there is an unmistakeable resonance within the messages. If we truly care about doing better by young working-class men in education, we must actively contest stereotypical assumptions and tropes which perpetuate systematically low expectations. Instead, we must replace them with the imperative to purposefully, and intentionally, listen. To connect with young men in ways which are authentic and meaningful, dispensing with what we think we know and replacing it with what we learn.

In the next chapter, we will explore just one thread in this complex tapestry of ways in which young working-class men experience education. A tapestry which, it saddens me to say, we still know far less about than we should. It will demonstrate what we can learn if we dispense with our preconceived notion of working-class boys as a homogenous group of young men characterised by a shared set of anti-school dispositions. The group of young men discussed in the chapter most certainly do not garner the same exposure as 'typical working-class lads' in media or political discourse, nor do they fit in with the stereotypical tropes and assumptions aligned with such preconceptions. It is a group for whom our current conversations, assumptions and actions in education and wider society do little to support. The next chapter will examine the educational challenges and affordances open to young working-class men who care.

7

Boys who care: masculinity, class and being a young carer

So far, I have gone to great lengths to challenge some of the common stereotypes surrounding young working-class men. To dispel myths surrounding an innate 'aggression, laziness and apathy' which are all too often attributed to the group with little evidence to justify the claims. Rather than continue to engage in conversation surrounding who they are not, this chapter takes a slightly different approach. It instead talks about who they are likely to be. Not from a place of assumption, but from one of evidence. It describes how these same 'disruptive' young men often hold responsibilities which directly contest the sweeping generalisations which are all too often made about them. That, as young working-class men, they are disproportionately likely to hold caring responsibilities for close family members within the home.

In the autumn of 2022, I was sat at a makeshift desk in my studio apartment, having an online meeting for work. As my job involves regular interaction with schools, colleges, youth, community and third sector organisations, I was chatting with a representative from a charity called MYTIME Young Carers.[1] Based in Dorset, MYTIME work to support young people who have caring responsibilities for a parent, sibling or close relative. As the meeting progressed, the face floating on my laptop screen went into a little more detail about what 'counts' as a young carer. By definition, a young carer is someone under the age of 18 who looks after close family members or friends. The caring responsibility may be due to a range of different challenges that the important people in their lives experience. It didn't just include young people who had parents with physical health conditions as I'd assumed but also individuals who struggled with their mental health and may be facing challenges due to addiction.[2] In other words, young carers were people who may have experienced similar things to me as a child.

For the first time, sat on an uncomfortable blue chair in a tiny flat at the age of 34, I realised that there were people out there who properly understood the challenges I experienced growing up. Not only were the difficulties of having a parent with issues related to mental health and addiction recognised, but there were charities set up to offer young people support. None of it existed when I was growing up as a teenager in the late 1990s and early 2000s, but over the last decade, through the work of organisations such as MYTIME, the issues faced by young people with caring responsibilities are increasingly being recognised and understood.

And it's a good job they are. The challenges faced by young carers in schools are significant. A 2023 report from an inquiry conducted by the All-Party Parliamentary Group for Young Carers and Young Adult Carers in England highlighted that:

- Young people with caring responsibilities have a higher prevalence of self-harm. Of children who do self-harm, young carers are twice as likely to attempt to take their own life as non-carers.
- Being a young carer has a knock-on effect on school attainment and attendance, with young carers missing 27 school days per year on average.
- Young adult carers are substantially (38 per cent) less likely to achieve a university degree than their peers without a caring role. Those caring for 35 or more hours a week are 86 per cent less likely.
- Young adult carers are less likely to be employed than their peers without a caring role.[3]

The implications of being a young carer, especially with regard to educational outcomes and mental health, are significant. Alongside this, the report highlighted that although the 2023 school census only identified 38,983 young carers in England, the real figure is likely to be far higher. A study conducted by the

BBC estimated that 10 per cent of young people in school had caring responsibilities.[4] In other words, roughly two young people in every class of 20 will be young carers. In 2016, the Children's Commissioner for England released a report highlighting the fact that just a small proportion of young carers across the UK were accessing the support they need.[5] Now, nearly ten years later, we've seen little movement at a national level to identify young people who may be engaged in care work in the home.

However, for those who have been identified, there is much more support than there once was. The Children's Society lead a programme with a national footprint,[6] working with partners such as MYTIME to champion the voices of young carers, calling for strategic action to be taken at a policy level to better identify young people who may be impacted.

Some 25 years after the fact, I realised for the first time that there was a way to articulate my experiences growing up with a dad who was fighting unseen battles. That there was strong evidence that my own challenges with mental health and school attendance were not individual anomalies. In fact, quite the opposite. They were shared by hundreds of thousands of young people in schools and colleges across the country every day. It felt a bit like someone had punched me in the stomach. In talks and workshops with young people, I often draw upon my own experiences as a youngster – they're a big motivator behind doing what I do. But talking about being a young carer felt different. It was much bigger, and at the same time much more focused. Playing that role within the household wasn't just part of who I was growing up; it was most of who I was.

Following my revelation, I spoke a little with the charity's representative and was invited to speak about my experiences as a panellist at a conference for educators that they were holding at a local university. Taking place in the university's largest lecture theatre, it convened hundreds of practitioners to discuss the specific challenges faced by young carers and what can be done to better support them. Getting up in front of people and talking a bit about my life and experiences doesn't usually faze me, but this time things felt different. I wasn't just speaking about my experiences as a young man – it felt like I was describing who I was. Honestly, it was one of the most difficult things I've done in a long time. Not due to MYTIME, the audience or the other panellists, all of whom were fantastic. It was due to having sudden access to a conceptual tool which was precise enough to dissect my experiences, analyse them and lay them bare. Unfortunately, I had reached this understanding just as I was opening my mouth to speak in a lecture theatre with 250 people staring down at me.

Articulating my experiences as a young carer growing up, I felt a surge of intense emotions. Ones that, when thinking about my childhood, I hadn't experienced in a very long time. Sadness about the pain the situation caused our family, and anger at how badly I was let down by our educational system. Shame. Shame about the things I did, shame about the way I thought and shame about the way I behaved while trying to navigate my way through it all. As is often the way with thoughts and feelings, they weren't entirely justified or based in fact, but when you rip off a plaster quickly, your first reaction is to flinch. And boy that flinch was a biggie.

From the conference, I learned two things. First, that coming to terms with adverse childhood experiences is best achieved with the help of a professional rather than 250 live spectators, and second, that I had access to a new lens through which to view and understand those experiences as a young man.

I came to realise that in the development of healthy masculine dispositions, being a young carer was a bit like having a secret superpower. Necessitated by looking after an unwell dad, I was given the space and opportunity to practise and develop emotional skills like the deployment of care and empathy. As a youngster, I'd become used to stepping in to mediate conflict in family arguments or talking my dad down from heightened states of emotional distress. I became very used to conversing with adults calmly in high pressure situations that, if not for my circumstances, I would otherwise have found very difficult.

Speaking to a range of health professionals to provide an assessment of a crisis incident isn't exactly what you'd expect to be doing while you're still in primary school. But I did, and it was valued. It provided a means to broaden and deepen my emotional literacy. Within my little family unit, kindness, sensitivity, empathy and connection were rewarded and encouraged. As a family, we needed it. Without it, I'm not sure any of us would have made it through.

However, I also learned very quickly that although these characteristics were cherished and celebrated within the home, they were not necessarily treated with such high regard in other places. In fact, in many other situations with friends or at school, they were the opposite of desirable. Displays of emotion which were not linked to anger or aggression marked you out as different. A deviant from the unspoken rules of masculine behaviour in the classroom and on the street. Visible demonstrations of sadness, fear or love were associated with being effeminate: a cardinal sin. They singled you out as a suitable candidate for social sanction. Verbal and physical abuse which could be deployed with surgical precision day in, day out. Your family, character and past actions would all be forensically examined for ammunition. Loaded into words and actions which could be used to hurt you. During my time at school, I vividly remember friends and classmates being tormented for having platonic friendships with girls, their parents' occupations, their weight, having a visible disability or coming from a family who couldn't afford new school shoes. If it elicited an emotional response from the target, it often intensified. Embarrassment and shame were weaponised to inflict the most damage possible. It damaged self-esteem, caused acute stress and eroded feelings of personal safety.

As a young man navigating this turbulent and often risky environment, not doing anything to stand out was often the safe bet. However, this also made you complicit. To fit in, you had to join in. I found myself divorcing who I was at home from who I became on the street, down at the park and in the school classroom. Kindness, care and empathy, attributes which I now cherish, were masked and minimised in an endeavour to feel safe and accepted. It's ironic that after spending much of my time as a teenager and young adult trying to eradicate these dispositions from my identity as a young man, they are now the parts of me which I embrace most wholeheartedly. These values form the foundational principles which underpin who I try to be as a friend, son, boyfriend and father.

Growing up as a young carer was difficult at times, but it instilled in me a set of core values which, although hidden for long periods, never really left me. When the shame of 'fitting in' and 'joining in' became too much, they were a place of sanctuary. A way to heal and start to make sense of what it all meant. I was afforded a rare opportunity, through necessity, to practise a different way to be a man. It helped me to recover my mental and emotional health, putting me on a path toward stronger, healthier relationships. I'm incredibly thankful that from an early age, I was taught how to care.

With an estimated 10 per cent of young people in schools engaged in caring responsibilities, the data would suggest that my experiences, while in the minority, were not unique. In fact, at my secondary school there were probably around a hundred other young men who were young carers within the home. Young men, now in their mid 30s, who never received the support they needed or understood what it meant for them.

Dan

Another individual whose caring responsibilities were hidden as a young man is Dan Morris. Standing at 6 feet tall and weighing over 100 kilograms, I would have had Dan pegged as working in sports coaching or athletics. But he doesn't. Instead, Dan's job is Head of Programmes for MYTIME Young Carers. Similar to myself, Dan's motivations for working at the charity are very much linked to his experiences as a young carer. Growing up in a working-class family, Dan's parents had him when they were aged 18 and 19. During our conversation, Dan explained how both his parents grew up in financially precarious situations and how, when he was young, he watched his dad build a business from the ground up. That was until his dad's battle with drug addiction took it all away.

Despite the challenges he faced growing up, Dan did well at school and was the first in his family to attend university. He largely attributes this to the remarkable determination and resilience of his mother.

Although he started his career in education as a primary school teacher, he struggled with the rigid systems and structures which accompanied teaching. When the job for MYTIME arose, he saw it as an opportunity to be more autonomous. It also directly linked to his experiences as a young man. During his time as a teacher,

Dan never made the connection between his own experiences and those of the young carers at his school:

> And as we went all the way back from my childhood, we ended up with the fact that I was a young carer. But that was never a term that I'd come across, and probably only ever came across it once or twice in my whole teaching career. Never had any input on it. There was a young carers group at my first school that I worked at, but I didn't really know anything about it. Just kids were taken out of my class, and then they came back.

It wasn't until a serendipitous meeting with MYTIME's chief executive officer in a coffee shop outside of a local gym that the conversation led to him joining the dots with his own experiences and those of young carers. It was a lightbulb moment. Many years later, Dan realised that he was not alone in his experience of growing up with a dad who battled with addiction. The realisation led him to apply for a job with the charity as soon as a suitable position became vacant, which resulted in our meeting a few months later. Now as a member of an organisation whose core purpose is to support young people who experience similar challenges, Dan leads on the development of their programmes:

> No one knew, no one knew what was going on at home. I lived with a heroin addict for about 12 years until my dad left. But yeah, I never spoke about home. Never spoke about life outside of school, just sports. Everything was sports orientated and that was an easy way for me to hide.
>
> I wasn't able to share what was going on. Mum just said you know, just go to school, behave, be neat and tidy. Don't draw attention to yourself. Come home.

During his time at school, Dan and his family took great care to make sure that his father's heroin addiction remained hidden. For his mum, it was important that Dan was well presented and didn't draw attention to himself through his behaviour. Due to his academic aptitude and love of sport, he describes school as a place he could unwind. Rather than it being somewhere he felt threatened or vulnerable, he saw it as a place of sanctuary. Because of his sporting prowess, he slotted easily into the 'peer group in school of the cool kids', using it as a scaffold by which to develop his identity. However, he never spoke with friends and teammates about life outside school. As well as boosting his popularity, he reflected that a love and aptitude for sport provided a convenient way to hide his home life from his friends.

Alongside popularity gained through his sporting involvement, another important way in which Dan maintained a sense of safety at school was a willingness to get into violent altercations should the need arise. While he explained that he was usually very calm, there were moments during his time at school where 'a red mist came in really quick, and it did end up in throwing fists'. As the eldest of three siblings, he reflected that he wanted to make sure he did everything a boy 'should' do. With a father who was engaged in his own struggles, he articulated how he felt that his role as the eldest son extended to the physical protection of his siblings and his mum. As such, he learned to box and regularly got into fights:

> I did everything a boy 'should' do when they're a kid, you know, learn to protect … I was very protective of my mum and my siblings as well. Got into lots of fights at school.
>
> And that's what I then found, probably my first elements of – I wouldn't say bullying – it wasn't bullying, but that like being left out. That was when it really kicked in, aged 14/15. That year nine, year ten, year 11 phase. I found a new friendship group, because I needed to find people who were a little bit more empathetic.

As his peer group progressed into adolescence, so did the behaviours and interests which were linked to status and acceptance. While Dan loved sport, he was not interested in smoking, drinking or the range of other activities which cemented the status of his peer group as the 'cool kids'. As such, Dan found himself drifting toward the social margins. He began to search for individuals whose values and interests more closely reflected his own. While, due to his reputation as someone who could look after himself, he never fell victim to bullying, looking back he identifies this period as a turning point. Many of his original friendship group went to work in the trades or service industries. However, for Dan, the social distance placed between them helped to cultivate the necessary conditions to set his sights on a different educational trajectory. A new, alternative path which involved continued educational engagement and aligned with his eventual participation in higher education.

During his time at school, Dan didn't consider his role to be that of a carer; rather, 'it was just the way that we survived'. Due to his lack of awareness that what he was doing at home constituted care work, he reflected that he never consciously negotiated challenges related to the tension between his caring responsibilities and masculine expectations among his peers: 'The fear that was sort of drummed into me from my mum about what could happen if someone found out; that was enough for me not to tell anyone. But for me it was like, you know, it's just what it is.' The need to hide what was going on at home allowed Dan the space to form an identity at school which was distinct and separate from that which he had within the family. He didn't recognise or associate the work he was undertaking at home as care. The detachment meant that his role didn't challenge his own perception of appropriate masculine behaviour or deviate from expectations which were present within his peer group. Instead, linking the activity to 'survival' affirmed toughness and fortitude, attributes held up as valuable characteristics for young working-class men to possess:

> I wouldn't say I suffered with mental health. What I did have though, were very niche quirks I developed that we would now probably link to mental health. I had a really, really, bad OCD [obsessive compulsive disorder]. Organisation, being on time, being neat and tidy. Even now, like today, we were chatting online, right? And I thought oh, we're going to be on camera, I've got to get a haircut!
>
> On reflection, there were many areas of my life that were very much out of my control. So, the things I could control, I had very tight control over. But if you compare that to the things that I was having to

do. Most of our evenings were spent driving around the local estate trying to find my dad's van. And I'm talking like two, three or four hours of driving with my two younger siblings and my mum, trying to spot his big work van so we knew where he was. That was something which was completely out of my control.

Although as a young man Dan demonstrated fortitude in spades, his experiences left a psychological imprint which he carried with him into adulthood. While he wouldn't describe himself as someone who struggles with poor mental health, he has nonetheless developed quirks which he directly associates with his experiences growing up. In a situation where, due to his father's addiction, there were so many things which were out of his control, Dan was fiercely protective of the things which he could influence. His meticulous organisation, timekeeping and care for his appearance were all mechanisms by which he maintained balance and a sense of control.

When Dan finished school and started his university studies, he specialised in sports coaching for young people. Later, he became a teacher and discovered a deep sense of purpose in helping young people develop the tools required to discover and critically engage with the world around them. When, at the age of 19, he entered his first classroom as a primary school teacher and found himself chatting with tiny young people, he felt very strongly that it was what he was 'put here to do'.

Examining his own experiences, he attributed his passion for working with young people to the sense of responsibility he felt for his two younger brothers. They were all quite close in age and went to the same school. While at numerous points during our interview Dan voiced the huge amount of respect and admiration he had for his mum, often she was preoccupied due to her full-time employment and dealing with the fallout from his dad's drug taking. As such, Dan assumed a level of responsibility for his siblings in school and at home:

I had my own expectations of what I thought a child could do, founded in what I did. So I had to learn to understand someone else's perspective and their story.

And it was a point of, like, well your story's not as bad as my story. You haven't got it as hard as I had it. That, that was a big thing, and I think that's the masculinity part in it as well. So, actually boys like you can get over this. But what I found is that these kids were never taught how to deal with these things.

During his early years as a teacher, Dan struggled with comparing his own experiences to those of young men who were exhibiting challenging behaviour. Due to the severity of the challenges he encountered growing up, he found it hard to understand how young men struggled to overcome difficulties which appeared to be less acute. Because fortitude and toughness were such foundational elements of his own masculine identity, it took a while to reconcile the experiences he had with those of the young people he taught. Interestingly, however, Dan attributed his development of such masculine attributes not to other men but to his mum. Highlighting the persistent role modelling of these characteristics by his mother, he now recognises the power of her influence in him developing such resilience. A resource which, on reflection, he realised that many young people may not have. As a senior leader in MYTIME, an organisation with a mission to support young carers who may share similar experiences to Dan's, he finds himself drawing regularly on his own experiences of navigating life and education as a young carer: 'There are a handful of lads who I talk to, and I think oh, that was me like 20 years ago.' Now approaching the challenges that male young carers may experience from a slightly more objective standpoint, he recognises the tensions linked to their negotiation of masculinity. The reconciliation of their caring role with the expectations they are trying to meet surrounding how a young man 'should' behave. When it comes to attributes such as empathy, care and compassion, Dan gives the example of one particular young man who 'knows he's got all of those skills, but he's not willing to own them. He'll own them in a safe space with us, but in his day-to-day life, he won't own them.'

For Dan, this reluctance to own and accept such attributes as part of a desirable masculine identity often presents a barrier to the young men being identified as carers in the first place. Of all the young people that MYTIME support, a large proportion are female. In early conversations with the young men, he reflects that often immaturity and silliness is deployed as a defence mechanism. It deflects attention away from the implications of their caring role. Of the physical and emotional work that they undertake in the home. It takes a concerted, sustained effort by Dan to engage with the challenges they might be experiencing and establish a great deal of trust before they're prepared to discuss them openly. In an effort to expedite the process, Dan often actively avoids the term carer in conversation with young men. Instead, he frames his engagement in terminology which he believes the young men may accept more readily: 'When I talk to young men now, I actively avoid the word carer. Maybe not avoid, but I try to get them to see it differently. Not you are caring, but you are keeping your family ticking over. Your family is succeeding, because of what you are doing.' While he has found this to be an effective mechanism to engage young male carers and build relationships, it is sad, nonetheless. For some of the young men he works with, there is such a resistance to the idea that caring is something that boys 'should' do that he abandons the term altogether. For the young men, it is probably not something they are even necessarily aware of. Fuelled by the unwritten rules of the social and educational spaces which they inhabit, a message that care is not a legitimate or desirable attribute for young men to possess is continually reinforced.

Dan's story resonated with my own experiences. While there are clear differences between us, not least half a foot and 20 kilograms, in places our lives were reflective of one another. We had a dad who struggled with addiction, we enacted two different versions of our identities inside and outside of the home and we were both very organised and punctual because they were one of the few things we could control. When deployed at work, that kind of understanding equips Dan with a powerful tool. Whether it be with myself or the countless young men MYTIME support, it generates empathy, trust and a deep sense of connection.

But unfortunately, Dan is just one person working for a single charity. When it comes to moving the dial on the way male young carers are perceived inside and outside of school, the resources of MYTIME pale in comparison to the task ahead of them. Making a significant positive impact on the challenges these young carers face involves a recognition that their lives, experiences and the integral role that caring plays within them are legitimate and important. An ideological shift in education and in wider society toward a notion that caring is what boys 'should' do.

Saul

One individual who understands the challenges faced by young carers inside and outside of education better than most is Professor Saul Becker. In terms of personality and appearance, you could not find two people who, on the surface, are more different than Saul and Dan. Saul is older, less physically imposing and carries with him an air of calmness and approachability. Within moments of meeting Saul, you get the impression that if he was one of your teachers at school, he would have been one of your favourites.

I met Saul at the same conference which initiated my own critical reflection on the role that care played in my life as a young man. At the conference, Saul delivered a keynote speech which provided a deep and detailed picture of the systemic challenges faced by young carers in the UK and across the globe. Following a serendipitous meeting up in Manchester several months later, Saul kindly agreed to be interviewed about his work. Through the conversation, I hoped to better understand the challenges faced by young carers in education and the part that masculinity played in his professional and personal life.

Initially trained as a social worker, Saul began research into the experiences of young carers in the early 1990s. In the intervening three decades, he has been engaged in over 50 research projects, written multiple books and delivered hundreds of conference presentations on the subject across the globe. As a result, he's firmly established his status as one of Europe's leading experts on the experiences of young carers. However, while his career is incredibly impressive, for the purposes of our conversation, I was most interested in how Saul's own negotiation of masculinity and caring responsibility influenced his life and work:

> My grandmother had Parkinson's ... I was then taking on the sole care of my grandmother. There was a

whole range of different caring tasks. It was sort of fetching and carrying and stuff, but then it became more intimate and personal. It included feeding her as she became more and more unsteady and disabled. And then there was the turning her at night. She would call out for help in the middle of the night so I'd go from my bedroom to hers. I'd have to help her into the toilet and wait to help her back into bed and things like that.

Saul spent large periods of time as a young man sharing caring responsibility for his grandmother with his mum. The experience of helping to manage the neurodegenerative condition, he reflected, played a foundational role in the development of his research interests and professional endeavours. From his perspective, it also meant that while he was conducting a significant volume of research, he was not producing knowledge which he saw as particularly new or ground breaking:

> I am proud of the fact that I say that my academic credentials are informed by my childhood experiences as a young carer, and I do think it adds a totally different perspective. So you know, I research and I find things; new knowledge. But it's not particularly new for me because I've experienced it. We call it new knowledge, but I've lived it, and so has every other young carer.

Although proud that his experiences have informed the vast amount of research he's produced, Saul views much of it as just validating what he and millions of other young carers already know. For Saul, this validation is important. The motivation for his work comes not from the 'production of new knowledge' but the opportunity provided through his work to give voice to those experiences which may otherwise remain hidden. His life providing care as a young man has informed his academic profile, the charities he works with and the values he has held close in his 30 years of research and activism on the subject:

> Caring roles and responsibilities shaped my identity as a child, and have had a massive, massive impact

throughout life. They've shaped who I've gone on to be in my professional life and what I've researched; but more importantly, much more importantly than what I've achieved, I think it's shaped my sense of my identity. Who I am and what I am. It's shaped my values and what I hold to be dear. I think it's also shaped my sense of my own masculinity actually.

I've been shaped by two people, both women, my mother. For my grandmother, I am a product of their values, and my grandmother was an immigrant to this country fleeing persecution.

The care that Saul provided from a young age was very different in nature from that which I had experienced. With my dad, it was predominantly on an emotional level, and my mum was nearly always around too. Saul's grandmother's illness meant that the caring tasks were often physical, sometimes intimate and personal, and there were times when he was providing that care alone. As the grandson of a Jewish grandmother who fled persecution and the pogroms of Russia/Ukraine, he was incredibly proud of the fact that his role models in childhood were both women. Although our experiences were very different, when Saul spoke about how his role at home had shaped his journey into adulthood, I once again felt that sense of connection. Care and kindness are something which he now describes as part of his DNA. They formed foundational principles on which his personal and professional life was built. In our discussion, he emphasised that his relationships with friends, colleagues, family members and romantic partners have been shaped by the care he provided as a young man.

However, the disjuncture between the caring he did in the home and the expectations surrounding masculine behaviour at an all-boys school in the 1970s meant his journey through compulsory education was turbulent:

Most people when I was at school didn't know that I was a carer … I had daily beatings for being Jewish for two years, and I was taken out of school by my mum. I then went back, but I've always had a very odd relationship with that school. I've only been back once in 50 years, and just to view it at a distance with no one else. The experiences were harsh, but the learning and education was good.

During his time at school, very few people knew that Saul was a young carer, or indeed what being a young carer even meant. Due to the regular physical and psychological abuse he received linked to his Jewish heritage, large portions of Saul's experience in schooling were characterised by trauma. Although still physically and emotionally demanding, his time with his mother and grandmother provided a measure of physical and emotional safety. Through the women in his life, and the activity he engaged in at home, he found solace in care. While Saul's time at school left him with psychological injuries which took a long time to heal, kindness, care and empathy provided a guiding light. His experiences as a young man being raised by 'two really strong women' left a distinctive imprint on his journey into adulthood. They've shaped the motivations, views and theoretical positions which he carries into his research as a university professor:

> I give a shit and I care. I like the fact that I will speak out for women's rights and experiences, but I will also speak out for boys' experiences. You know, it's just that my sense of identity is very much more located in experiences which have traditionally been gendered as female so it is complex, really complex.

In our conversation, Saul reflected that traditionally, research concerning informal family care had focused on work undertaken by adult women. Due to the disparities in the division of domestic labour, and the resultant inequalities experienced by women in the workplace and the home, it had become a primary focus of feminist research and campaigning over the last half a century. However, Saul's early research provided a platform to begin a slightly different conversation. His work demonstrated that not all carers were adults. It also challenged the inherent assumption that this group was mainly made up of women. In his early work conducting surveys with young boys and girls who were caring at home, Saul explained that the gender gap between those identified was incredibly small, 'literally only a few per cent'. His work uncovered that when it came to young people, there were large numbers of boys who were also engaged in work as carers:

> If family structure is just a girl, or just a boy. One daughter, one son. It doesn't matter what gender they are, they are the only available person to care. They are elected into that role because they are there and they are available. Gender is important, but family structure is critical. Family income is critical. Gender is important, but not in itself a determining factor at all.

Due in large part to necessity, if care was needed, and a young man was the only person available to undertake such activity, then they would inevitably fulfil the caring role that was required of them. In exposing the comparative balance of responsibilities for young carers across genders, Saul's work also exposed how it cut across gender taboos. In our discussion, he provided examples from his research of young men's involvement in intimate care for their mothers. How providing personal care and performing tasks such as taking their mum to the toilet could result in humiliation for both parties, alongside having longer-term implications for their psychological and emotional wellbeing. While the division of caring responsibilities played a critical role in the entrenchment and reproduction of gender-based inequalities across wider society, in Saul's research gender played a greater role in understanding how such work was experienced. As he reflected, 'in terms of determining who is likely to be a young carer, gender would not be at the top of the list':

> Most of the research has pointed toward young carers coming from lower-income families. And that's in a way almost among the bleeding obvious because if a family has illness, long-term disability impairment, drug addiction, mental health, etcetera … We know that the incidence of mental health among adults is much more likely to be higher in low-income families.
>
> For young carers there's a massive correlation between socio-economic disadvantage and being a

carer. Those disadvantages will cast their shadow not just through childhood, but into their own adulthood. That's proven through multiple research studies and increasingly longitudinal datasets.

Instead, he suggests that a more useful indicator of who is likely to be a young carer could be found in those who experience socio-economic inequality. Research suggests that impairments to mobility linked to disability, and struggles with addiction and poor mental health, are likely to impact a far greater proportion of individuals from working-class backgrounds. So, as Saul so eloquently puts it, the fact that young people from these backgrounds are also likely to be young carers is 'bleeding obvious'.

While in other chapters we have explored issues related to masculinity and inequality in education more broadly, Saul's research touches upon their intersection with caring responsibilities. If a young person is already in a position where they have unequal access to social, cultural and economic resources due to their financial circumstances or ethnicity, Saul explained that in education, the responsibility for care can have a compounding effect. This additional layer of complexity extends the depth and reach of existing inequalities, alongside presenting new barriers and challenges:

> It's difficult for any young carer, actually, irrespective of gender or gender identity, to say that they're a young carer at school. It's been a real problem. Many young carers are simply not identified in school or anywhere because it's a secret and invisible life. The vast majority of young carers will never be known to educators.

One such challenge, Saul explained, related to a lack of awareness among educators about which young people held caring responsibility within the classroom. Issues such as lateness, school absence, lack of concentration and falling asleep in lessons, or refusal to give up a mobile phone, were all too often attributed to purposeful poor behaviour. They resulted in punishment and sanction for young carers, coming as a direct result of the responsibilities they held at home. While awareness around young carers is growing, he still feels that such missteps from educators in classrooms are happening all too frequently:

> They might be judging their behaviour if it's a boy as 'bad boy behaviour', you know a problem with boys. But it might not be a problem with boys and gender. It might be a problem that they're a young carer, providing multiple hours of care before and after school and they're totally knackered, frankly. So when they're at school, what they are doing is regarded as 'boy behaviour', but you have to look behind it because it's not the cause.

For boys in particular, Saul spoke of the risk that behaviour deemed unacceptable in the classroom would be incorrectly attributed to anti-authoritarian attitudes. Due to ingrained stereotypical assumptions surrounding young men in the classroom and expected 'laddishness', he worried that there was a disjuncture between the explanation often given for such instances and the actual cause. As highlighted earlier in the book, research suggests that the perceptions and expectations of educators surrounding working-class boys' engagement in education are important. Indeed, they may be one of the most significant contributors to disparities in educational attainment and progression. For male young carers, such assumptions may result in punitive action being taken in place of much needed understanding and support.

Alongside challenges relating to their engagement with staff, Saul asserted that young carers were also more likely to experience bullying than their peers. Due to the navigation of significant responsibilities at home, opportunities to spend time with classmates or friends could be extremely limited. A set of circumstances which, if experienced for a prolonged period, can perpetuate feelings of exclusion, isolation and vulnerability. At its worst, it can heap the risk of physical and emotional harm at school on top of the significant load of psychological strain that young carers already experience:

> He was a boy caring for a mother. When pupils found out that he was a young carer, they really laid into him

in terms of bullying. If I recall rightly and, as I say Alex you can look it up, they actually set fire to him. They also called him gay; he wasn't gay, he was just looking after his mother. But they thought that that must make you gay. Because he was caring for his mother, they conflated gender identities, caring roles and sexuality into a violent package for this kid. Was he gay? No, he was a boy looking after his mother, but for this he deserved to be bullied and set fire to.

The case study Saul is referring to is from a 2008 report entitled 'Young adult carers in the UK' in which a 19-year-old young man provides an account of his experiences in school.[7] The passage describes how deviating from activities which were expected of a teenage boy from a working-class background made him a target. He spent his free time outside of school cooking, cleaning and looking after his parents at home '24/7'. When combined with the fact that he was overweight, he explains how the 'weird' behaviour he displayed in not drinking or going out in the evening placed him in a vulnerable position with his peers. It led to verbal and physical assaults from fellow students targeted at his sexuality and 'manhood', beatings and, in one instance, being set alight.

This example is perverse, ridiculous and tragic in equal measure. Thankfully, it is also a rare and extreme example of the type of bullying that a male young carer may experience. However, it is also illustrative of how the intersection of masculine expectations and social class can play out for young carers inside and outside of school. When combined with the challenges Saul discussed in relation to teacher perceptions of young carers' behaviour, it paints a rather bleak picture. However, since the 'Young adult carers in the UK' report was written there has been significant progress to increase the visibility of young carers in education as well as the challenges they experience and the support available:

It's incredibly valuable for society. It has an economic cost for the child, but it's incredibly valuable because we are understanding, teaching, nurturing, encouraging and celebrating the value of care. The alternative would be to have kids who have no sense that care is important. I can assure you that our classroom will be a hell of a lot harder to manage than the ones in which we recognise young carers. I've made the point before, but it would be a horrendous classroom wouldn't it, if we didn't celebrate care and kindness.

For Saul, this progress is important. While his primary motivation is to ensure that young carers receive better support throughout their educational journey, he believes that this support has the power to achieve something far greater. What support and recognition for young carers boils down to is the recognition in education and wider society of care, both physical and emotional, as legitimate, valued and valuable.

As discussed at the start of the chapter, the characteristics I developed through the responsibilities placed on me within the family as a young man are ones which I now consider to be my greatest strengths. As a man in his mid 30s, working with young people who experience marginalisation in education and wider society, care, compassion and empathy are tools I draw on every day. When focused outward, they help to build and maintain happy, healthy relationships, support others in the workplace and at home and build trust with young people who encounter significant challenges in their day-to-day lives. However, I'm able to do so from the privileged position of being at incredibly low risk of anything bad happening as a result.

As a White middle-class man with 'Dr' in front of his name and a cushy, permanent job in education, I now live and work in a context where such dispositions are accepted and celebrated. However, with that awareness comes an acute recognition that it is a later-in-life luxury afforded to very few young working-class men. In Dan's reflections of growing up as a young carer, we saw how during his formative years the caring responsibility he held within the family remained hidden. We also saw how even now in his work for MYTIME, he is reluctant to use the term 'carer' in his engagements with young men for fear that such a label would impinge upon his ability to build trust and rapport.

Through the conversation with Saul, we gained an understanding of the instrumental role his caring experiences played in shaping his identity and the motivations behind his research. He shone a light on the significant proportion of young men who undertake unpaid care work in the home nationally, explaining how, as a group, they often go through the education system undetected. The consequences of this lack of awareness, he argued, were significant barriers faced by young people with caring responsibilities both inside and outside the classroom. For male young carers specifically, the challenges were further compounded. Saul spoke of educational settings where displays of care constituted legitimate grounds for harassment. In these spaces, caring was effeminate, at odds with what it meant to be a 'proper' young man. It made them a target for bullies, adding weight to the already-heavy burden of responsibility they carried.

For Dan, Saul and myself, the caring roles we were required to take up as young men played an instrumental role in shaping who we were and who we went on to be as adults. It provided us with the tools to navigate psychological and emotional challenges and led us into work which actively drew on the characteristics we acquired. However, those experiences were also a source of trauma. They compounded other inequalities, increasing the risks we faced when, as young men, it came to abiding by unwritten codes of masculine expectation. In much the same way as it still does for millions of young working-class men across the UK, our lives and experiences as young carers were hidden. Disguised under a camouflage of bravado and performative action. A camouflage that while safeguarding our physical and emotional wellbeing, meant that the challenges we faced went unnoticed and unsupported. For young working-class men, the responsibility for care of a loved one may be just one element of an identity which is complex and multifaceted. You could easily substitute being a young carer for a range of challenges. They could have a parent who is in prison, they could have been placed in foster care or they could be going back to homes with no power, heating or access to the internet. These challenges, and the stark absence of understanding in conversations surrounding support, illustrate a pressing need to dispense with what we think we know about what being a young working-class man is like and start listening to those who do.

Being a Boy: learning from the real experts

While it's my hope that the conversations which have taken place so far have been interesting, it is also hard to escape or excuse the fact that, up until this chapter, none of the voices heard within the book come from individuals under the age of 30. In other words, the people interviewed in this book are recounting experiences of boyhood which involved calling people on landline telephones, using Ceefax to get the football scores and buying a disposable camera to take on holiday with you. A different world. While many individuals have conducted research or work regularly with young men, none of our voices can speak with the authority of lived experience. An expertise on what it's truly like to be navigating adolescent life as a working-class young man today.

In a post-pandemic Britain, currently undergoing the greatest cost-of-living crisis of a generation, the edges of socio-economic inequality are sharper and the cuts are deeper. With the rise of the manosphere and social media influencers such as Andrew Tate,[1] working-class boys' place within society is constantly debated and discussed by the media, politicians and educators alike. Within all of this, there is a notable lack of space given to the voices of those who feel the consequences most keenly, the real experts in what it's like to navigate these challenges: the young men themselves.

So, at my place of work, a small university specialising in creative subjects on the south coast of England, we decided to do something about it. My job at the time was Access and Participation Manager. I led a team tasked with providing opportunities for young people to engage with creative subjects who, due to their school curriculums or experiences of inequality, may not otherwise have had the opportunity. We also supported slightly older students to successfully apply to study at the university. At our institution, young men make up just over a quarter of the total student population. Students who were eligible for free school meals (FSM) account for a small proportion (about 11 per cent) of that number.[2] It's fair to say that, like the creative industries employing our graduates, at the moment it's a largely White, middle-class campus. But we're doing our best to change that. So, in late 2021, we devised a pilot project for young working-class men called Being a Boy.

When it comes to GCSE grades, as an educational institution which specialises in creative subjects, we're not equipped to run tutoring programmes in maths and english with young men in schools. Nor should we. There's plenty of other universities that are better placed to do that type of thing than mine. So instead, with Being a Boy,[3] we decided to play to our strengths. As we've covered at length, problems associated with the educational outcomes of working-class boys have been studied, articulated and re-articulated for years. They also haven't provided a clear direction on what can be done about it. We know that issues related to socio-economic inequality, normative working-class masculinities, peer pressure and teacher expectations all combine to contribute to disparities in educational attainment and outcomes – but how did this *actually* play out in the experiences of a young working-class man in Dorset in 2022? We thought Being a Boy could be a tool to find out. Using creative writing, photography and dance, the project mobilised the subjects as mechanisms for the young people engaged to conduct their own reflections on what being a boy meant to them. The students attending the workshops were from a mixture of mainstream schools, alternative educational provision and community partners, with the project being open to all students who met the eligibility criteria and identified as a boy. The boys wrote poems and raps, took photographs and put movement to music, creatively exploring identity, masculinity and how being a boy influenced the perception of their place in the world.

The rest of this chapter recounts the experiences of three young men from a local alternative education provider who, over the course of the project, I've been privileged to get to know. The names of the three young men, and the educational institution they attended, have been anonymised. It tells the story of Fear, Geo and Jay, describing what happened during their time with the project and sharing their reflections on what took place.

I first met the boys about three years ago. After a meeting with the Careers Leader from Seaside Academy, the provider of alternative educational provision we'd reached out to about the project, we'd arranged for an initial conversation with some of the students who might be interested in creative workshops. Nestled in a town near the Dorset seafront, the school is located just a stone's throw away from popular tourist spots and two-bedroom seafront apartments costing upward of a million pounds. With steadily increasing numbers of young people being permanently excluded from mainstream education since the pandemic,[4] the lives and experiences of Fear, Geo and Jay contrasted starkly with those holidaying in the apartments just down the road. Each of them faced a range of challenges linked to social and emotional wellbeing, mental health and caring responsibilities in the home. The tangled web of challenges they faced had converged to mean that, by the time we met them, they were part of a group of young people studying at the alternative provision.

Sitting in a small meeting room just down the corridor from the main reception, a colleague from the university and I waited for the young people to arrive. Slowly, over the next ten minutes, they filtered into the room. In doing so, they had been pulled out of lesson and placed in front of us with very little context other than being told they were going to talk with two complete strangers from a local university about 'doing art'. Outside, it was pouring with rain. While introducing ourselves, sentences were punctuated by the squeak of wet trainers on the floor, and silence. It was awkward. Given our respective positions, we'd have been naive to expect anything different. They were a group of young people who had been repeatedly let down by educational structures and systems in a multitude of different ways. They had been mistreated, excluded and marginalised. We were from a university, a place that extended formal education for another three years. A place where people were *charged money* to continue learning in a system which had done nothing but fail them. If we had carried any assumption into the space that the young men had good reason to listen to what we had to say, we'd have been misguided.

As the meeting went on, we started listing the different courses and different bits of technology and equipment the university had on offer. I talked a little bit about my own experiences growing up. How annoyed I was about people not getting access to different opportunities through no fault of their own and invited them to come and have a go at whatever they were interested in. After about 20 minutes of forced conversation, a small group of students agreed that they'd quite like to give our virtual reality design software a go. So, after the meeting, we set up their first visit.

This visit, which included Fear, Geo and Jay, was the first of many to the campus over the next two years. We slowly got to know each other. Often, they would just pop in for a hot drink, lunch and a chat. Other times, it was for a workshop or to find out more about a specific subject area. Trust started to build. The young men knew they could opt out of anything they didn't want to engage with. The power was in their hands. I slowly found out more about them, their lives, their hopes for the future and the issues they grappled with both inside and outside of education. After our fourth or fifth meeting, I spoke to Jay, Geo and Fear about the Being a Boy workshops. They agreed to take part.

Alongside the lads from Seaside Academy, there were several other young people engaging in Being a Boy from a variety of mainstream schools and providers of alternative educational provision. 'Empower' was the first workshop. A day of creative writing and performance led by the author of *Wild East* Ashley Hickson-Lovence.[5] Growing up as a working-class teenager in London, Ashley's own experiences have been instrumental in shaping his career as an author and his perspective on inequality, masculinity and education. It's his fundamental belief that lived experience, mixed with creative writing, is a powerful vehicle for self-expression. He's also one of the most talented facilitators I've ever been in a room with. Prior to the workshop, we had been told by numerous parties that the boys involved 'wouldn't last 45 minutes writing, let alone a whole day'. They were wrong.

The atmosphere was electric. A stark contrast to that rainy meeting over at the school only a few short months earlier. For a full day, the young men wrote poems, raps and creative pieces.

They focused on what it meant to be them. Ashley introduced them to examples of writing from published authors, and they used the pieces as stimulus for their own. Not only did they write; they also performed. They stood up in front of their peers and read excerpts that were funny, moving and, at times, deeply personal. The following piece is written by a young man who used the poem 'I come from' by Dean Atta as inspiration.[6]

I come from

I come from a small house on a busy road
I come from constant arguing
I come from memories with my family
I come from not enough sleep
I come from not being able to stay calm
I come from doing stupid stuff with people who
  I thought was my mates
I come from breaking things
I come from overcoming my fears
I come from learning not to judge others till I walk
  in their shoes
I come from.

In academic circles, research has suggested that a real challenge of work with young men centres on a willingness to talk about thoughts and feelings that may be uncomfortable.[7] Yet, as demonstrated in the poem, this didn't seem to be the case within the security of the environment created by Ashley's workshop. In the piece, the young man speaks of family conflict and arguing, struggling to control anger and the effects of peer pressure on his actions. He talks about the lessons he's proud of learning. Overcoming his fears and the value of empathy. He didn't just write the poem down; he stood up in front of a room full of young men and read it out. He had the bravery to be vulnerable.

The poem succinctly describes the relationship of the young man to the social conditions in which he lives. How his family, his friends, his house and his home contribute to the formation of his outlook on the world and the way he behaves. It contrasts significantly with overly simplistic, stereotypical narratives which constitute the outdated 'taken-for-granted' assumptions about young working-class men. Narratives which, as we have previously discussed, individualise the damage dealt by societal inequality. The wealth of newspaper articles, media clips and speeches by politicians which heap the weight of responsibility for its consequences on to the shoulders of these 'deficient' young men.

Instead, the poem shines an honest light on the lived experience of the young author. Its truth, its nuance and its complexity. He considers how the physical, social and psychological conditions he navigates are negotiated and incorporated into his sense of self. He describes the challenges he faces, and those shared by young men like him, with a depth and eloquence which, all too often, is profoundly absent in government and media discourse about masculinity, education and inequality. It's a case in point of how wildly superficial and inaccurate broad-brush, stereotypical assumptions around a lack of 'resilience' or 'aspiration' can be.

How to be a boy

1. Don't beat yourself over small mistakes.
2. Don't overcook yourself.
3. Don't get discouraged or start to lose hope when your thoughts get scrambled.
4. When you meet new people don't be afraid to break the tension with some conversation.
5. Life can get heavy, don't let it weigh down on you.
6. Don't let your emotions get mixed up.
7. Combine your brain and brawn to get the best out of yourself.
8. Try not to let your blood boil.
9. It's OK if you knead to take a break.
10. Don't let your dreams dissolve.
11. Don't be afraid to mix it up.

However, the creative writing also demonstrated that those assumptions, alongside the narratives arising from them, had snaked their way into the young men's perception of themselves. The poem in the previous excerpt was written collaboratively by a group of three of the workshop's participants. In this exercise,

Ashley had introduced them to the concept of list poems, and they were asked to devise a piece of writing titled 'How to be a boy' using cooking metaphors.

What is immediately striking within the piece is how many of the instructions begin with or contain the word 'don't'. Out of the poem's 11 lines, it appears in eight. The prevalence of the word points to feelings of responsibility for constant vigilance against problematic behaviours; behaviours which are inherently linked to their identity as young men. Lines such as 'try not to let your blood boil' speak to struggles with difficult emotions such as anger and the expenditure of emotional energy needed to keep them in check. Lines such as 'don't get discouraged or start to lose hope when your thoughts get scrambled' speak to confusion and the implications of negative thoughts and feelings for their self-efficacy. It places the idea of the future as something which is at risk. A place in which their dreams and aspirations could easily dissolve.

The dominance of anger across the two poems is also apparent. Although it is clearly a problematic emotion for the authors to negotiate, it is one which is readily discussed. While its inclusion in the poetry is upsetting, it is perhaps unsurprising. In a patriarchal societal structure, anger is afforded legitimacy as one of the few forms of emotion which is 'acceptable' to display in front of other young men. It was a topic which could be discussed in the writing without risk of social sanction or judgement from peers. Yet it is a microcosmic illustration of the double bind these young men continually attempt to manoeuvre within.

As discussed earlier, displays of anger and aggression may be tools which provide status among young men. In my own account, and those of others, there have been examples of how anger can be used as a protective shield. A way to keep safe from the immediate risks of physical and psychological injury that may be present within the day-to-day educational experiences of a working-class boy. However, it also inflicts harm, stifling more productive forms of emotional expression and perpetuating feelings of guilt, shame and hopelessness. It is an emotion which boys are simultaneously encouraged to display and punished for displaying. One which bestows masculine status but at the cost of psychological injury. It engenders respect and security among peers but leads to punishment in education, relationships and wider society. The poem quoted earlier speaks to the authors' negotiation of this psychosocial paradox and their efforts not to lose hope in the process.

While not featured in full, in another poem using cooking metaphors, the words of the young men suggested an exploration of their aspirations, desires and who they might like to be in the future. However, they were almost always tempered by pragmatism. Lines such as 'don't let your dreams dissolve' and 'chop your brilliance to smaller expectations' suggested a disconnect between their hopes and ambitions and what they saw as realistic and achievable. The young men made reference to future selves which were desirable but needed to be 'chopped' down into something they could expect to accomplish. Not a lack of aspiration, but realism. An honest reflection on their material conditions and whether they could expect their aspirations to be realised. For those who maintained hopes and ambitions for the future, their words imply a fragility. A risk that, even though they hold on to them, without constant vigilance their dreams could dissolve.

Sitting at the back of the room while Ashley's creative writing workshop was taking place, I reflected on just how different it felt. The energy. The young men's willingness to engage deeply, meaningfully and openly about their experiences. Although, as demonstrated through the conversation with Mike Nicholson earlier in the book, there are small pockets of activity which engender this type of response in education nationally, it is by no means commonplace. With Ashley's skilful, energetic and caring use of creative writing, we had stumbled upon a key which appeared to unlock confidence and vulnerability in self-expression. But how did it work and why?

To answer that question, I went to our real experts. The boys themselves. A few months after the first Being a Boy workshops, I went back to Seaside Academy to speak with Jay, Geo and Fear about their experiences. By this time, I'd known the boys for about a year, and they agreed to take part in some interviews. After an initial meeting to explain the research, see if they wanted to take part and agree parental consent, I returned a couple of weeks later. Armed with some their favourite snacks and a dictaphone, we talked about what taking part in Being a Boy had meant to them.

Following the interviews, I sat down with Dr Jon Rainford,[8] a colleague and an expert in education, inequality and access to higher education from the Open University, to make sense of what it all meant. Alongside the activity with the young men, Jon and I had been working together to evaluate the project, alongside doing some academic writing.[9] Given that a wealth of wider research has illustrated the problematic nature of ideas linked to an 'aspirational deficit' among young working-class men,[10] we took a different approach. Using a concept called *possible selves*, we sought to understand how Jay's, Geo's and Fear's experiences influenced their thoughts and feelings about education and their future within it.

Based on the work of psychologists Markus and Nurius,[11] and more recently developed by educational sociologists such as Holly Henderson,[12] the concept of *possible selves* provides a tool to more deeply understand how people might perceive the future based on the complexity of their identity and lived experience. It's an experience which is formed in a continual, ever-evolving relationship with the social settings and circumstances they might find themselves within. Through this relationship, work using *possible selves* suggests that individuals develop a palette of like-to-be or like-to-avoid selves based on what they see as probable.[13] In other words, they position what they could reasonably expect to happen in the future based on the social, cultural and economic resources made available to them in the present and the past. Their access to these things is influenced by a plethora of elements including friends, family, peers, educators, their geographic location and their material circumstances. As a tool, it is by no means perfect, but it affords the opportunity to understand the boys' reflections with a level of nuance which is often starkly absent from this type of work.

As well as the snacks and the dictaphone, I also brought with me the range of creative artefacts they had produced during their time taking part in Being a Boy. It included pieces of writing they had authored in Ashley's workshop and self-portrait images they had taken of themselves during a day which focused on photography. The following passage is a result of their reflections on the pieces. It captures some of their experiences and their thoughts on what life is like as a young man who has been excluded from mainstream education. Jay, Geo and Fear are not directly attributed to any of the quotes from the interviews, but the rest of the chapter is my best attempt to platform their voices. Their position as the real experts in all of this. By drawing from mine and Jon's research in creativity, education and social inequality, it also makes links with the wider challenges they navigate. Barriers, often submerged just below the surface, which are negotiated in continual dialogue with the educational and social settings which shape their experience. Jay, Geo and Fear provide depth and clarity. Real life, contemporary examples of how their thoughts and feelings link inextricably to the uncomfortable truths. Jarring lessons that we, as men in society, must acknowledge and learn from if things are to change for the better.

Protecting yourself and avoiding harm

A core theme generated from our conversations with the young men centred on the idea of protection from harm. During the photography workshop, participants were asked to strike poses which represented how they feel young men are viewed by society. Across the images taken were a series of poses which appeared confident but were also guarded. In several of the images, there were stances and postures which were reminiscent of boxers or mixed martial artists. It suggested a preparedness, a readiness to contend with harms that were often projected on to them by society. Commenting on a particular image in which his fist was visibly clenched, one of the young men related his physical gesture to other situations where he may feel the need to adopt the same pose:

> I also find myself sometimes like having a tensed fist, like a closed, fully closed fist and I don't know why. My friends notice it all the time when I'm walking down the road with them and my shoulders are up and my hands are like, if my hands are like that and they're like my thumbs in my pockets and like tensed fists and they ask me they go like, 'Why do you do this?' I genuinely don't even realise I'm doing it … Sometimes I think it's more of a … in some sense

like a survival kind of thing, because especially living in rough areas you don't know if a person is going to come up and try and start on you, and having a closed fist definitely gives you that thought of I'm going to be ready in case anything happens. More than if you have like open hands at the sides, or were walking with your phone in your hand.

He associates this clenched fist with being physically prepared. Not metaphorically for harms that are projected by society but for 'survival'. Living in a rough area of town, he talks of a constant state of vigilance. A readiness for physical harm which may befall him. That even an activity as mundane as walking down the street is one which requires being constantly prepared for an altercation which could end in violence:

> I went out with my friends, and they got into a fight with someone and they hit them and he was unconscious on the floor and I was the only one that was freaking out because I didn't think he was breathing and he was bleeding from his face. You know and then obviously everyone was videoing it because it was in a public area, and people were on their phones and obviously they, they made us run away. One of my friends like dragged me away from the thing … I think it's just seeing a person there knowing that my friend had done that. It's the thing definitely which made me cut off contact with them eventually, but it's just knowing that they could do something like that.

Later in the conversation, the young man explained how, after the incident, he tried to cut off contact with a friend who had taken a central role in the fight. As a result, a new set of consequences emerged. While he spoke of feeling sure that it was the right thing to do, and being encouraged by adults that he trusted to do so, he developed a new set of anxieties about running into his old friend while he was out. By trying to protect himself from similar traumatic experiences in the future, he had positioned himself on the outside and feared the repercussions: 'I was in the right for breaking off contact with that person. Yes I saw them for a little while after that like in passing and you know they'd laugh and they'd like shove me but other than that it stopped after a while.' In this account, the social ramifications amounted to insults and shoving; however, they could often be more severe. Another of the interviewees spoke of how, even though they had no desire to get into a fight, they felt pressured by those around them to engage in public displays of violence:

> Even my friends that I've had since I was about four years old right have just said, 'Hit him', to me and I was like, I was like I don't want to hit you, there's no point. If I'm going to hit you it's going to be on my terms and it's going to be for something that you've done or said that's really, really got to me because I'm not, I'm not really that type of person.
>
> It's definitely there that everyone wants you to fight someone and some people have even told me to go pick a fight with a random person because they want entertainment. I was like I'm not going to entertain your childish wishes because you want to see me get hurt.

These young men, teenage boys no older than 15 years of age, describe a choice they were relentlessly being asked to make. A choice between violences. A decision between harming others or causing psychological, emotional and sometimes physical injury to themselves. Often the only options they felt were available led to a situation where both happened. These encounters and actions weren't isolated or detached from their day-to-day lives; they were moves in a game of ever-growing complexity, one in which the stakes were their health and their happiness.

Alongside it came a continual negotiation of difficult emotions. As explored in the 'I come from' and 'How to be a boy' poems earlier in the chapter, anger was an emotion which they negotiated frequently and expressed regularly. It was one of the few emotions they were 'allowed' to have. The way the boys described dealing with anger varied across the interviews. While some found talking helpful, even though it was a difficult thing to do, one of the

young men recounted how, when it got too much, he would
vent his feelings physically:

A: I've just got better at controlling anger.
Me: In what types of ways, how?
A: So my desk at home is a unit, got a few drawers and
   cupboards, and I just hit the drawers in a massive
   blowout every now and then.
Me: OK does that mean they're quite dented now?
A: No, they're made of wood so it's really strong.
Me: Doesn't that hurt your hands though?
A: Well, I've gotten used to it now.

For this young man, negotiating the consequences of his anger
was something he felt that he should be able to handle alone. An
emotion that he should take sole responsibility for dealing with.
He described how he did so by directing his aggression toward
his bedroom furniture. The feelings were channelled physically,
hurting him as a result. The conversations with the young men also
implied that means of self-expression which were less damaging,
such as talking openly or writing things down, would be risky.
This was especially evident when it was considered against their
day-to-day experiences in the classroom. During an interview,
one of them hypothesised what would happen if they wrote down
or shared some of the creative writing he composed in Ashley's
workshop during a 'normal' day in his class at Seaside: 'I feel like it
would be used more against me. I feel like you know, the bullying
and torment would definitely go up quite a bit for I guess, you
know, something stupid like writing how I feel on a page.' He
was sure that, within his usual educational context, writing down
his thoughts and feelings on a page would present a risk to his
wellbeing physically and emotionally. Choosing words like bullying
and torment, he describes the potential repercussions of actions
which fell outside of what was 'expected' for young men in his
day-to-day educational context. When considered in relation to
the quote from the young man about hitting his cupboards, we
once again see these young people caught up in negotiations of
risk which placed them in a zero-sum game. They either expressed
themselves in a 'healthy' way, and in doing so risked greater threats

to their physical and emotional wellbeing at the hands of their peers; or, on the other hand, they conformed to what they felt was expected of them as young men in their social and educational context, running the risk of hurting themselves in the process.

Safety in self-expression

In their day-to-day experience outside of the home, Fear, Geo and Jay felt there was very little freedom to express thoughts and feelings when it came to being a boy. There were tightly bound expectations surrounding masculinity and their identity which they felt pressure to adhere to, even though the consequences were undesirable. But, as touched on earlier, this wasn't the case for Ashley's session and some of the other Being a Boy workshops. The atmosphere was markedly different. In contrast to the risk that came with self-expression in the classroom context, one of the young men commented on how comfortable he felt:

> I think it was just the general atmosphere of the room. You know no one was really jokey, and honestly like you know, they didn't really care that I'm from a different school, they don't care why I'm there. You know they're there for their thing, I'm there for mine.

When discussing his overall impression of the creative writing workshop, the lack of concern about what other young men in the space thought about what he was saying, doing or writing was evident. It wasn't a space in which 'banter' dominated. The fun wasn't laced with threat. He didn't feel judged, either by the young men who went to Seaside or by other young men that he didn't know. The reflections positioned the context and atmosphere of the workshop in stark contrast to their experiences in school. For another of the young men, this was due in large part to the facilitator:

Me: So what did you think of Ashley as a teacher?
A: Really good, involving everybody and everything.
Me: Is that what made him good?
A: Yes, and he's a good chatter. He takes his like view and changes it with other people's views.

Me: Was it the same as like the type of stuff that goes on here, or is it different?

A: No, it's different.

Me: Like in what kind of way?

A: Because Ashley pretty much makes our view become his view while he learns, while our teacher just makes us do work.

Reflecting on the differing styles of practice between Ashley and the teachers at his school, they felt that there was a key difference in the nature of the relationship. Due to Ashley's own experiences navigating the education system as a working-class boy, and his passion for creative writing, he viewed engagement with young people as a privilege. This comes through strongly in the quoted discussion. Rather than Ashley's knowledge or expertise being placed upon a pedestal as 'holding most value', the workshop was a conversation. A dialogue in which the views, opinions and ways of describing the world were shaped together to arrive at a shared understanding. This practice of teaching and education, this pedagogy, is by no means a new phenomenon. Its transformative power in education has been widely discussed by leading thinkers and practitioners such as hooks,[14] Freire[15] and Henry Giroux.[16] Its engaged, relational nature supported the young men to feel that the experiences they brought into the space were a valuable part of the learning process. They were not empty vessels to be filled but agents whose experiences were valued and integral to the process. Ashley and the young men were learning together. The poems demonstrated a willingness to reflect on aspects of their lives and selves which the boys' reflections illustrate would have been difficult outside of the comparative safety of the workshop setting. With the openness of expression came a deep reflection surrounding thoughts and feelings they found challenging. Something which, as highlighted by Jay, Geo and Fear, was not something that they often felt they were afforded the freedom to convey.

Pride in their accomplishments

Some of the creative artefacts that Jay, Geo and Fear spoke about with most pride were the self-portraits produced as part of the photography workshop. The photos clearly denoted exploration and experimentation. They played with different lighting, poses and stances. Often during our discussions about the images themselves, it was a challenge for the young men to provide a concrete rationale for the choices they made. However, they were incredibly proud of what they produced. In the following snippet of conversation, one of the young men talked about how the images were exhibited at home on his bedroom wall. The fact that he'd laminated them for protection and displayed them prominently suggested that for him, they carried a greater value than just another 'set of pictures':

Me: Whereabouts are they the pictures now?
A: In my room.
Me: Have you got them on the wall?
A: Yes.
Me: That's cool.
A: I got it laminated which was really helpful. Because if they weren't laminated, they were just going to fall off.

It was clear that the work they had produced as part of Being a Boy was important to them. Their involvement in the project provided an opportunity to engage with a new and different type of educational experience in a different educational setting. Prior to meeting the team and engaging with the project, none of them had been on a university campus. In the following quote, one of the young men describes how the visits misaligned with his preconceptions about what university was like: 'Yes, bigger than I thought and more things you could do there. Because for an art university I thought you were using like paint and that, and that's it. I didn't expect moulding, combining pictures, photography, all of that, I didn't expect that for art.'

At Seaside, due to limitations with curriculum and staff, there was scarce opportunity to try different creative subjects. He voiced his surprise at the large variety of different disciplines which fell under the umbrella of 'art'. Visiting the institution unlocked an awareness of the broad suite of creative educational possibilities that were available. Instead of art being synonymous with stuffy art galleries, paint and canvas, it now involved numerous, specific subject areas which all counted as 'art'.

A: I liked it a lot because I cannot wait, this year I get the book finally.
Me: Oh do you.
A: Yes, I cannot wait because I'm still upset that I couldn't have it last year.
Me: Well [staff member] has got it stored away for you.
A: I keep on reminding her and making sure she doesn't forget it.

Following Ashley's creative writing workshop, the participants were also given a signed copy of his first published book, *The 392*.[17] Given the book's content, it was agreed with staff at Seaside that if they weren't already, they could have it once they turned 15. Often with workshops like this, the excitement quickly fades once young people put some time and distance between themselves and the day. However, one young man who was 14 at the time of the interview spoke of his excitement to receive the copy which was being held for him by a staff member at his school.

Alongside voicing excitement at getting his hands on a copy of the book, he spoke enthusiastically about sharing his work with his family at an upcoming celebration event organised by the university:

A: My mum is excited to see what I've done.
Me: Yes, does she see much of your kind of schoolwork and stuff?
A: No, because we don't have parents' day here I don't think. I'm not sure though I think she might have seen some of my work in primary school and that's it.

Having been excluded from a more mainstream educational setting, he reflected that there was little opportunity for things he did in class to be a source of celebration. There was a palpable sense of pride when he spoke about his mother's excitement to see the work he'd produced as part of the project. Interestingly, although Fear, Geo and Jay articulated their experience of the workshops as very different from that of their normal classroom, they still framed the creative pieces they produced as 'work'. However, rather than it being 'schoolwork' they had been made to do, it was something they had invested themselves in working to produce. It was a clear source of pride.

For another of the young men, the impact of the workshops was less about what was produced and more closely bound to feelings of confidence and self-worth:

> I actually find myself now thinking you know, when I get scared of something, get scared of talking to a new person, or jumping off of a small cliff into water with my friends, you know I kind of think back to the university project. Like I was scared of going and you know I was scared of meeting the new people and doing all the new stuff and now I think back to it it's like I done it. If I can do that, I can do anything.

At the beginning of our time together, he described how his engagement invoked a fear of trying new things and meeting new people. However, he took part despite his misgivings. The young man describes how the experience with the project is one which he now draws on when encountering new situations that are difficult. While for other young men there was a sense of pride in producing and displaying the physical pieces from the project, for him the sense of pride came from an internal change. He felt he could draw on his experiences to navigate new social settings which he may find intimidating or unfamiliar.

Negotiating the possible

From the snippets of conversation with Jay, Geo and Fear detailed in the previous section, it is clear that their involvement in Being a Boy had an impact. It provided an opportunity to participate in education creatively and differently. Through the relationship built with facilitators such as Ashley, they engaged deeply. They explored issues relating to their identity, masculinity and the future, expressing them in ways which may have otherwise been difficult. It provided an outlet for them to articulate the pressures, risks and complexities that are entwined with their experiences as young men in education. An experience which, as described in their words, is often fraught with risk. Within the fragments of conversation, discussion and reflection, we can see how, for some of them, their involvement provided a means to reconsider preconceptions around who they are and who they 'should' be. For others, it created the conditions in which their thoughts and feelings were both valued and valuable. As young men who for a variety of reasons had been disengaged or marginalised in more formal educational settings, the fact that it was not like school was important.

Practically, it also offered insight into what a creative arts university is and what it offers. From the university's perspective, this is the goal of outreach work. However, how meaningful could it really be when held up against the totality of their time in education? As a slight diversion from hundreds of hours in a classroom which provided a very different message about the value of their experiences, their intellect and the possibilities for their future? Exposure to an environment where they could enjoy writing and creatively experiment may have challenged perceptions. Indeed, for one of the young men it may have even sparked an interest in reading for pleasure. But, within their day-to-day educational context, how many experiences such as these are likely to be replicated?

This brings the challenges faced by these young men, both inside and outside of the school classroom, into gut-wrenching focus. An environment where continual vigilance is required against threats to their physical, psychological and physical wellbeing. Harms which were as likely to manifest from the inside as the outside. Where a sense of safety is only ever a peripheral figure, and the tools provided to navigate their way through school life are blunt and broken. Stuck in a set of structural conditions where they are simultaneously encouraged and sanctioned for the same behaviour. Where in poems about their lives, what they 'can't' or 'shouldn't' be appears in nearly every line. Where brilliance needs to be chopped down, and dreams are under constant threat of dissolving.

No matter how effective they are, a set of workshops can't tackle this. It would be like trying to stave off a tsunami with a sandcastle. After the workshops, Fear, Geo and Jay still went back to a school which offered the opportunity to study three subjects at GCSE, in a region where fewer than two in ten young men who are eligible for FSM will obtain a grade nine to five in maths and english at GCSE. If we are to tackle this collectively, we need to think about what can be done on a much, much larger scale. A sentiment which leads us nicely into the next chapter.

9

Boys' Impact: a roadmap to hope

As the Being a Boy project drew to a close, I felt proud of what we'd accomplished. It would have been naive to expect it to achieve any more than it did. In many ways, the enthusiasm displayed by the young men while engaging in the pilot surpassed our expectations. But deep down, I knew it wasn't enough. It was one small change within a landscape dominated by unhelpful assumptions, practices and stereotypes. When combined with the inequalities these young men experienced, the educational challenges they faced were substantial and complex. The project was a brief flash of luminescence. A feeling of understanding and connection to these young men who had put their trust in us when they had no good reason to. We felt a deep sense of pride in curating a set of conditions in a space of learning where they felt valued and valuable. But it was also limited. Limited in duration, limited in frequency and limited in resource. When considered against the sheer scale of the pitfalls baked into the educational and social ecosystems surrounding them, the colour quickly faded.

Years of living, learning and working have been a catalyst, enabling me to form a deeper appreciation of these ecosystems and their impact on the educational experience of working-class boys and young men. Building on that knowledge has become my vocation. For the last decade, I've been leveraging every tool at my disposal to better understand what's going on and why. So, when we began work on Being a Boy, it was from a place of expectation that this moment would come. That the difference we could make conducting a small project at a small university on the south coast of England would be restricted to the resources we had at our disposal. Even before my first meeting with the young men from Seaside in that small meeting room on a rainy day in 2022, I knew that the issues we sought to engage with were far, far bigger than any one individual or organisation could address in isolation.

However, Being a Boy didn't run in isolation. It ran in parallel to a significant body of research and practice taking place across the UK. Activity which sought an equitable alternative to the deficit-laden discourses which, over the course of decades, have morphed into taken-for-granted assumptions about working-class boys in education. Projects which disrupt the notion that you must be White to be working class. Initiatives that addressed issues related to misogyny and gender-based inequality as readily as disparities in educational attainment through targeted, strengths-based work with young men. A movement toward a new mode of practice which, as highlighted by Mike Nicholson earlier in the book, didn't care *what* these young men wanted to be but instead focused on *who* they wanted to be.

When it comes to educational research, one of the leading figures in work aligned to such an ambition are the Taking Boys Seriously (TBS) team.[1] Having been engaged with work on issues related to masculinity and educational inequality for nearly two decades, I first became aware of the TBS project nearly five years ago. While I had been working small, they had been thinking big. Conducting research with nearly 1,000 young men in education during that time, the TBS team have developed a strong understanding of the challenges they face. From the evidence, they have also developed some very good ideas around how to address them.

Upon reading the TBS research, it felt like I had been provided with the missing piece of the puzzle. A means to better understand the experiences of the young men on the Being a Boy project. A way to contextualise their experiences within a wider educational ecosystem, and a mechanism to shift the focus on to their relationship with the educational locations they inhabited. Since my first meeting with Susan who heads up the TBS team several years ago, they have been instrumental in developing my capacity to extend thinking into the bigger picture. Through their work, they have provided us with perhaps the most important tool. A way to think beyond reflections on the 'attitudes' of individual students in individual schools. The research, and the conceptual tools built around it, have provided us with a means to take a step back. To examine the wider social and educational contexts young men operate within and develop a holistic understanding of the young men's experience based on their relationship with them. When combined with what we have already learned, it provides the first draft of a blueprint. A roadmap toward a model of practice which is characterised by hope.

It's a framework which demonstrates a potential for making that splash of luminescence we experienced on the Being a Boy project larger and more permanent. A guide for how collectively, we can cultivate an educational climate which gives primacy to the relationship between educators and the young men they educate. This final chapter will lay out a plan. A vision for what a new, educational ecosystem could look like. But to begin with, we'll start by taking boys seriously.

Taking Boys Seriously: employing the principles of relational education

Based in Northern Ireland, the TBS team, led by Susan Morgan at Ulster University, are nearly two decades ahead of where we are in England. Established in 2006, TBS was initially a longitudinal research project co-funded by the Northern Irish Departments of Education and Justice.[2] It was a project designed to work alongside adolescent boys and educators to promote the conditions where they flourished in a diverse range of educational settings.

As an investment in educational communities across Northern Ireland, the team have developed strong partnerships with local schools, youth centres and community organisations. Fostering collaboration between settings of formal and informal education, they work to address disparities in outcomes for young men which present in a very similar way to our own.

Using the phrase 'compounded educational disadvantage' to describe the challenges facing young working-class men in education, they use the analogy of a backpack. Through the legacy of historical conflict, a system of selective education, normative masculinities and experiences of relative poverty, the TBS team describe the systemic issues as bricks which are added to the metaphorical backpack of a young working-class man, making their journey through education more difficult.

Rather than focus solely on the young men as individuals, it is the relationship of these issues with their educational ecosystem which is of primary interest to Susan and the TBS team. As opposed to layering the young men thick with the tar of individual aspirational and educational deficiency, it is a recognition of their place within this ecosystem that lies at the heart of their work. To date, their research has engaged with over 800 adolescent boys and 200 educators across 45 formal and informal education settings.[3] It has constructed a dialogue with young working-class men and their supporters, with the foundations laid in boxing clubs,[4] community centres[5] and schools.[6] Through their work, they have developed a new model of engagement with young men centred on ten principles of relational engagement:

1. Recognise the primacy of relationship
2. Demonstrate dignity and respect
3. Utilise a 'strengths-based approach' to learning
4. Challenge and affirm masculine identities
5. Promote positive mental health
6. Identify blocks to boys' learning
7. Connect boys' learning to context
8. Engage meaningfully with boys
9. Enable creative learning environments
10. Value the voice of boys[7]

A full description of the TBS principles, alongside indicators which enable educators to gauge whether they have been implemented successfully, can be found in the Appendix. However, I have included an illustrative example of the first principle below.

1. Recognise the primacy of relationship

While these principles are to be viewed holistically rather than in a hierarchy of importance, recognising the instrumental nature of the relationship between young men and their educators feels like a very good place to start. In a recent study including data from 442 adolescent boys, the TBS team reported that they spoke highly of educators who connected with them, listened, and understood their point of view. Of teachers who challenged them, but in a supportive way.

Within this principle, and the data which underpins it, is an understanding that, contrary to stereotypical assumptions, boys are not a homogenous group. Instead, they have a breadth and depth of skills, experiences and interests which make each young man unique. In applying the first principle, an educator understands this, developing a relationship which places a young man at the centre of their learning. The relationship is one which emphasises positive working alliances and high expectations for what the young men can achieve in education. Indicators of success include young men reporting:

• a renewed sense of belonging in education;
• increased confidence about their knowledge and learning;
• educators showing an interest in them and their lives;
• feeling more comfortable seeking personal and educational support;
• perceiving learning as being essential for their future opportunities.

Based on a body of research and evidence spanning nearly two decades, the work of Susan Morgan, Dr Andrew Hamilton and the TBS team at Ulster University has provided us with an invaluable gift: a starting point. Through their rich, deep, long-running exploration of the challenges faced by working-class young men in education and wider society, they have cultivated fertile ground for growth and development. That is not to say that the journey is complete; far from it. If that were the case, there would be no need to continue writing this book. However, the TBS principles provide us with the tools required to begin the process of growth. To think about how they might meaningfully and intentionally be applied in transformational practice. A new mechanism to build and sustain relationships with young men in settings of formal and informal education which look different. Perhaps most importantly, TBS have also gifted us with an evidence base from which to articulate the impact of our efforts.

In the previous chapter, I introduced you to some of the young men who took part in Being a Boy. If you look back, there is clear evidence of the TBS principles at play. Within the structure of the activity, and the reflections of Fear, Geo and Jay, we can see how principle 8 (engage meaningfully with boys), 9 (enable creative learning environments) and 10 (value the voice of boys), were operationalised throughout the project. However, as discussed earlier, the activity constituted a flash in the pan when considered against their day-to-day experiences as young men in education. No matter how engaging the sessions, how interesting the content or how rich the conversations, it wasn't enough. It couldn't be. We needed to do more, to work with educators, schools and community organisations to figure out how we could change the day to day. Susan and the team at TBS talk about their work in education as the creation of ecosystems. Of initiating cultural change which is embedded into the fabric of these contexts through the intentional use of the principles. I began to think about how, at a local level, we could achieve this. At around the same time, I was incredibly fortunate to bump into an educator by the name of Deneen Kenchington at a conference.

Boys' Impact

Anybody who has met Deneen will testify that she is an absolute force of nature. The Deputy Headteacher of Ferndown Upper School, a medium-sized secondary school in Dorset, she is possibly even more passionate about this subject than me. When I first met her, she was busily conducting her own research into the experiences of young working-class men in education as part of a qualification she was studying for alongside her full-time job as a school leader. At the time, I mentioned to her that we were running a project at the university, and it would be fantastic if some of her students wished to attend. What happened over the next two years was quite incredible.

Through a series of excited conversations and introductions to key figures like Susan from TBS, we worked in partnership. Using the gifts Deneen brought to the table, she began to reflect on what the application of the TBS principles would mean when applied to her school's teaching and learning, safeguarding or behaviour policies. Using a shared language, we were able to augment the herculean task that Deneen had undertaken in reviewing her school's strategies with the creative activity we were undertaking at the university. In my role as a researcher/practitioner, I plugged Deneen into networks which held different opportunities for her students. We began getting in front of people. Actively engaging with any educationalist in the region who would listen to us about what we were trying to do. Conversation by conversation, we built a local coalition of educators who were willing to try a new, evidence-based approach to improving the educational outcomes of young men who were eligible for free school meals (FSM) in their local contexts.

As time went on, we were able to articulate the impact of the work with young working-class men at the school more clearly. In our second year, the attainment gap between young men and women who were eligible for FSM at the school closed, incidents of 'disruptive' behaviour decreased and permanent exclusions went down. In the case of Deneen and the school, we had evidence that the intentional application of the TBS principles, alongside a range of supplementary interventions such as our creative Being a Boy project, 'worked'.

Our relentless banging on the doors of regional school leaders began to bear fruit. We spoke at local headteachers' conferences and initiated conversations with those involved in educational policy. However, it still wasn't enough. While the transformation Deneen had instigated in her school was incredible, there is only one Deneen — both in terms of her passion and her deep understanding of the issue. So, we began to think about how we could use our experience to support local school leaders in a more structured way. Between us, we came up with an idea: Dorset Boys' Impact Hub. The hub was to be a local network of educators who were committed to proactively engaging with the challenges young men face linked to masculinity and inequality in schools. At our first meeting, which included senior leaders from 12 educational institutions, community and third sector organisations across the region, we introduced the TBS principles and set them a challenge: to pick a measurable impact that they wanted to see for the young men in their charge and intentionally apply the principles in support of achieving it. Rather than basing activities on stereotypes and assumptions about what 'young men need', we provided them with the means to start a different conversation. A way not only to select interventions which addressed the most pressing issues within their local context but a means to understand the impact it had for the young men as a result.

As I write this, the Dorset Boys' Impact Hub is still very much at the beginning of its journey.[8] We don't know how successful our application of the TBS principles will be, but we've made a solid first step toward finding out. The now 30-strong group of educational practitioners have begun supporting the development of our local ecosystem and piloting work in their own contexts. In July 2024, Bournemouth University ran its first 'Dorset Takes Boys Seriously Conference'.[9] It brought together 150 young working-class men from schools across the region for a day of inspirational talks and workshops aligned to TBS principle 10. A local educational partnership made funding available to support in school pilots of projects aligned to the TBS principles. One local school bid successfully for funding, ran a pilot project and has seen a statistical improvement in attendance and a reduction in internal exclusions experienced by young men at their institution as a result. At a local level, we have begun to cultivate the ground of our educational ecosystem with activity we can learn from. Next year, we have secured funding to run targeted pilots based in nine of our local partner schools. Each will be mobilising the TBS principles, and each will be sharing what they have learned along the way. We are slowly, step by step, building an understanding we can use to drive forward the development of our practice in the future. Viewing the challenges that young men face through a different lens, we intentionally use the TBS principles, measuring their impact in addressing issues linked to attendance, behaviour and attitude to learning. We have begun to see, through a plethora of different means and mechanisms, how the cultures in our local schools and community organisations can begin to evolve.

But, in much the same way as our university project was a drop in the ocean compared to the young men's day-to-day experiences of education, so is Dorset when compared to the United Kingdom as a whole. To develop impactful strategic activity which has the chance of working as well for young working-class Black men in London as it does for young working-class White men in Newcastle, we need to think bigger. We need an approach which uses the shared language of the TBS principles but has the flexibility to meet the needs of communities in very different local geographic, social and historical contexts. There needs to be an overarching organisation, a body which can act as a convening force, providing infrastructural support to regional hubs in areas where geographies, histories and social contexts are different. Like Dorset, each hub would be populated by local experts. Schools, youth and community organisations who understand the region and the challenges faced by young men within it. A network which creates a tangible impact for boys and young men by embracing their world.

What we've done so far constitutes a start. Between 2022 and 2024, we held conferences in Bournemouth, Manchester and Wolverhampton, convening educators from across the UK to deepen their knowledge on issues impacting upon young working-class men in education. At our last conference, nearly a third of the delegates were headteachers and deputy headteachers from schools across the country. Through discussion and collaboration, a movement is starting to grow. A coalition of educators, community practitioners and researchers, spearheaded by a network called Boys' Impact. Founded in the autumn of 2023, Boys' Impact is still in its infancy,[10] but it holds significant potential to enact meaningful change at scale. We don't have any funding, and work to develop the organisation is largely done by volunteers after work or at weekends. But for me, that's a real strength. People are contributing not because they are set to make any financial gain but because they care deeply and want things to change for the better. It's generated a palpable sense of energy. A tangible desire by a collective of educators to make a positive difference to the future health, happiness and opportunities of young working-class men. Not as young men whose decisions, views and actions float free of the educational and societal structures which influence them but as individuals in continual dialogue with the environments which shape their dispositions. A conversation in which they use the resources and opportunities available to them to cultivate behaviours, attitudes and orientations toward education and wider society. This approach isn't seeped in individual deficit. Instead, it recognises the role of societal structures in limiting the emotional growth of young men, narrowing their field of vision and the spectrum of future opportunity available to them. It embraces the innate richness and diversity in their experiences, seeking not to pathologise them but to celebrate what makes them unique. A shameless focus on the aspects of themselves that they are most proud of. It offers a mechanism by which to unlock new ways of thinking, exploring where those thoughts could lead with curiosity. To feel connected, empowered and walk with pride toward a future characterised by healthy, rewarding relationships with themselves and others.

We are at the beginning of a journey, one characterised by hope and a stubborn optimism that things can be better. An endeavour which, if supported, holds the power to be transformative. Transformative in classrooms, transformative in communities and transformative across wider society. On the ground, it begins with piloting many, many more targeted interventions with young working-class men in settings of formal and informal education. Using the TBS principles as a starting point, we will need to be bold. As educators, we need to be open to the idea that the conditions we create for working-class young men in the classroom are as important as their interest in the subject or their initial eagerness to learn. Above all, it requires a relentless focus on the *how* rather than the *what*. With careful thought given to programme design and evaluation, it provides an opportunity for schools, community and third sector organisations to articulate not just that something has worked but how and why. In short, we will collectively begin to plug the chasmic gap in knowledge and understanding which constitutes our evidence base for what effective practice looks like. With it, we can move forward with purpose.

It will take time, but while it builds, we can explore other possibilities which complement and augment our endeavours. What would happen if the TBS principles were used to inform training modules in initial teacher training? How could pre-existing organisations like the Chartered College of Teaching[11] or large multi academy trusts with schools across the nation mobilise, support or develop mechanisms for large-scale pilots or teacher training? In other words, how can we bring this all-important ecosystem together nationally as robustly as we have started to within local educational contexts?

To do so, we'll need support from policy makers. Those who, on a day-to-day basis, very few of us engage with, but who hold the power to accelerate the fantastic work which is already beginning to take place. Over the course of the last eight chapters, the book has engaged with people and organisations who are quite extraordinary. Men and women who are relentless in their mission to equip young working-class men with the tools required to support their journey toward a future characterised by healthy relationships and positive outcomes. They work tirelessly, deploying mechanisms in research, pedagogy and practice to foster a set of conditions where the lives and experiences of marginalised young men are held as valued and valuable. While we're still at the start of a very long road, it is a hopeful beginning for education, and one which is brimming with potential.

10

Conclusion: The will to change

While the conversations taking place within this book have by no means been comprehensive, they have opened the door to a different perspective. Whether the lens has been directed toward the consequences of socio-economic inequality, mental ill health, education or young men who care for their loved ones, it reveals a picture of depth and complexity. An understanding which emphasises the power and importance of an individual's material conditions, geographic location and their place within history. It demonstrates how, instead of being atomised, peripheral considerations for young working-class men, these issues stitch together, informing attitudes and perceptions which influence actions taken in the 'here and now'. The book examined how the collective memories of communities and geographies provide a foundation on which this 'here and now' is built. An interweaving of societal and educational structures that lay the groundwork for perceptions of what it means to be a man successfully, to form. Across generations, these structures have placed unrelenting pressure on the shoulders of working-class boys to become 'real men'.

Often using family homes and school classrooms as the sites in which these unwritten expectations are transmitted, the implications were evident in my own journey. A baton of intergenerational trauma and mental ill health that was passed down from my grandfather to my father and then to myself. The intergenerational nature of the issues discussed, to some greater or lesser degree, has threaded its way into many of the conversations recounted within this book. We observed it through

the words of Steve Roberts, Mike Nicholson and Mark Roberts
when describing their own negotiations of masculinity and social
mobility. In a more contemporary educational context, we also
heard it in the experiences of the young men who participated in
the Being a Boy project. When it came to attempts to break this
cycle, all the conversations were characterised by the same things.
Risk, threat and the avoidance of harm. A constant weighing
up of the lesser of two evils. A choice between conforming
to expectations or facing the consequences of deviation. In
different situations, spaces and times, we have seen how social
and educational ecosystems work to make young working-class
men players within a zero-sum game. Gambling their health,
wellbeing and educational outcomes on a dice roll in which there
is little chance to win. When faced with such a choice, decisions
are predicated not on the chances of success but on limiting how
badly you lose. Safety at the expense of learning, a dopamine hit
of acceptance at the expense of your self-worth. Each time the
stakes are raised, and the consequences become more acute.

These ills are the dual edges of a structural sword which cuts
both ways. For women, battling against the severity of social,
psychological and physical harm caused by patriarchal societal
systems has been a struggle fought by the feminist movement
across generations. However, as described so succinctly in J.J.
Bola's book *Mask Off: Masculinity Redefined*, it is this same system
that puts men at an advantage in society which 'limits them,
inhibits their growth and eventually leads to their breakdown'.[1]
Through research, interviews and illustrative examples, we have
seen how this is the case. How these same structural forces cause
psychological, emotional and physical injury to young working-
class men. It has facilitated a deeper understanding of the all-
important *why*. Why men, particularly those from working-class
backgrounds, are less likely to 'succeed' in education and more
likely to experience a range of issues including mental ill health,
addiction and substance misuse, entry into the criminal justice
system and death by suicide.

Rather than being separate from, or in opposition to gender-
based violences which perpetuate these ills, they are results
of the same societal machinery. A behemoth which has been
churning out the same pernicious product across generations. Our

conversation has highlighted how, if we talk of these challenges as though solving them is simply a case of 'fixing' individual young men, we miss the point. Rather, the words of this book call for a deeper consideration of the mechanisms by which social inequality, and problematic elements linked to masculine identity, persist across time and geography. It's been an invitation to think about what we can, and must, do differently.

All young men, regardless of their ethnicity, geographic location or socio-economic circumstance, deserve the chance to look hopefully upon the person they can expect to be in the future. An expectation that they will be happy, healthy and secure. A future in which they are great fathers to their children and capable of maintaining rich, trusting relationships with the people they love. One where the tonic to their sadness isn't a bottle of whisky, and the salve to their insecurities isn't anger and violence. We can create those conditions. Pockets of hope for a future like this are stitched into the chapters of this book. They are in the thoughts, feelings and actions of men and women who have recognised the damage the status quo is doing to us and are actively working to change it.

But the task ahead of us is significant. It will take a new approach, cultivating new ecosystems in health, education, work and the home which embrace a new understanding. A deep appreciation of the relationship between individual young men and the social world they inhabit. Of the instrumental role played by the systems, structures and cultures that young working-class men navigate. How both are shaped in a continual dialogue with one another. If meaningful progress is to be made, this relationship requires an unrelenting focus.

However, there are significant obstacles. When we consider mainstream media and political discourse, such an understanding is starkly absent. As demonstrated at numerous intervals throughout this book, the disparity in educational outcomes, and the wider harms associated with normative working-class masculinities, for men and women, have been documented for decades. Yet within the societal stories told, the issues have been held as separate and oppositional. Narratives from the political right claim that 'young working-class men have been pushed out due to feminism', while narratives from the political left characterise young working-class men as 'perpetrators of misogyny in waiting'. Such polarised views, framed as binary, 'either/or' explanations, rob us of the ability to engage in constructive, meaningful, dialogue. A way of engaging in conversation which may lead to finding a middle ground or reaching consensus.

The truth is that these issues aren't simple. Just like the society in which we live, they are wickedly messy and complex. And when socio-economic inequality is added into the mix, they become even more so. In education, it's easy to appreciate that a figure of 17 per cent for boys who are eligible for free school meals achieving a grade nine to five (A★–C) in GCSE maths and english in my local region is horrendous. But when it's entangled within a web of wider issues surrounding gender-based inequality, it can get lost. Especially when gendered disparities in educational outcomes are mobilised by agendas seeking to sow controversy and division. We get drawn into the simplistic. An alluring binary of either/or explanations which hold little in the way of meaningful or productive explanatory value.

While the policy makers and media moguls delight in the political points they have scored and the reposts and mentions they have achieved, it comes at a very real expense. The expense of a mechanism to build a future where our young men can expect to lead happy, secure and fulfilled lives. Journeys into adulthood in which they are less likely to contribute to the horrendous statistics cited in this book and more likely to be compassionate, empathetic individuals with healthy, loving relationships.

In a landscape full of polarised rhetoric, social media trolls and deep political division, the prospect of sticking to these tried and tested oppositional narratives can be alluring for politicians. It's a darn sight easier than doing something different. Putting your head above the parapet and publicly voicing a different position constitutes a risk, a deviation from the consensus. It makes more sense to wait for someone else to say it. To play it safe until a silver bullet arrives. Something which will hold guaranteed votes at the next election, tackling the issues quickly, efficiently and with minimal fuss.

This book contends that if that is what we are waiting for, we'll be waiting for a very long time. Not just years, but decades. And while we wait, my child will grow up in a world in which the hope for something better is starkly absent. Not because we can't do better, but because we won't.

However, we are fortunate to live in a society which isn't completely dominated by those holding the polarised viewpoints I have described in this chapter, even if they are those which are most commonly cited. Alongside the groundswell of activity taking place at grassroots level through organisations such as Progressive Masculinity, MYTIME, Future Men, Taking Boys Seriously (TBS) and Boys' Impact, through the cracks of old, tired stereotypes surrounding masculinity and manhood, we are beginning to see small shoots of change and growth in the public imagination.

Conversations which were once locked tightly in the ivory towers of academia are slowly finding their way into podcasts, radio programmes and television shows. Discussions which are increasingly being led by men, and even on the odd occasion, one from a working-class background. In April 2024, there was a two-part documentary on Channel 4 which engaged with masculinity in the 21st century called *How to Be a Man*,[2] hosted by famous actor and TV personality Danny Dyer. At around the same time, the BBC launched a short documentary series on Radio 4 called *About the Boys*.[3] Rather than content based on tired tropes and stereotypes, the programmes were concerned with listening. While by no means perfect, the issues affecting young working-class men were approached with a genuine curiosity in which developing a deeper understanding appeared to be the primary aim. The BBC show even interviewed the TBS team. In the spring of 2024, the UK Parliament's Education Select Committee put out a call for evidence, launching an inquiry into the 'Underachievement of Boys in Education'. Although the title of the inquiry made me cringe for numerous reasons, it was the first indication of a willingness by policy makers to listen. Unfortunately, due to a general election being called in the UK on 22 May,[4] the inquiry was dissolved and is yet to be reinstated.

Although small and incremental, I am hopeful that these are the early signs of a long overdue change in our public conversation. A movement away from the divisive, simplistic and reductive, toward a landscape in which a different dialogue about masculinity and societal inequality can begin. One which is motivated by the need for constructive, productive conversation; a new model of shared understanding which recognises the role of collective memories, communities and geographies. Discussions which generate a shared appreciation that, while young working-class men are part of a patriarchal system which benefits them in numerous ways, they are by no means the 'winners'. It creates conditions in which the opportunities for young men to learn intellectually and emotionally are limited. Their capacity to care and be cared for, slowly chipped away by the relentless pressure which constitutes normative masculine expectations. That there are two edges to this sword, and that both truths are capable of being held simultaneously.

If instead of confidently stating that the solution to the crisis of mental health in men is for them to simply 'talk to their mates more', or writing off young men who may be acting out in the classroom because 'boys will be boys', what would be possible? If rather than pathologising working-class young men as individually deficient of aspiration and moral value, we instead took a step back and examined those educational and societal interactions which sculpted their expectations, what opportunities would this new understanding afford? If we consciously challenged our taken-for-granted assumptions surrounding the things working-class young men wanted to learn, the jobs they can do and the type of man they can become, how would our relationships with those young men change?

Instead of a debate which continually creates an either/or binary between work to support young men and young women, what if we worked harder to understand the ecosystem in which their attitudes and future perceptions are shaped together? If we promoted early years education and care work as a possible career to young men, as vociferously as we promote STEM careers to young women? Not because those sectors need 'male role models', but because they are sectors where emotional intelligence, care and empathy are among the most prized attributes for a professional to hold. If we started from a position which challenges our gendered assumptions and collectively recognised that the status quo is hurting everyone, what would be possible?

As I reach the end of this book, it seems fitting not to do so in my own words but rather those of American author, theorist, educator and social critic bell hooks. The following is a quote from her book *The Will to Change: Men, Masculinity and Love.*

> To truly protect and honour the emotional lives of boys we must challenge the patriarchal culture. And until that culture changes we must create subcultures, the sanctuaries where boys can learn who they are uniquely, without being forced to conform to patriarchal masculine visions. To love boys rightly we must value their inner lives enough to construct worlds, both private and public, where their right to wholeness can be consistently celebrated and affirmed, where their need to love and be loved can be fulfilled.[5]

While I, and the other contributors to this book, will continue doing our part in education, perhaps if policy makers heeded the sentiment, we could all move toward a set of conditions where the future for young working-class men and women alike looked a little more hopeful.

APPENDIX

Taking Boys Seriously principles

1. Recognise the primacy of relationship

While these principles are to be viewed holistically rather than in a hierarchy of importance, recognising the instrumental nature of the relationship between young men and their educators feels like a very good place to start. In a study including data from 442 adolescent boys, the Taking Boys Seriously (TBS) team reported that they spoke highly of educators who connected with them, listened and understood their point of view. Of teachers who challenged them, but in a supportive way.

Within this principle, and the data which underpin it, is an understanding that, contrary to stereotypical assumptions, boys are not a homogenous group. Instead, they have a breadth and depth of skills, experiences and interests which make each young man unique. In applying the first principle, an educator understands this, developing a relationship which places a young man at the centre of their learning. The relationship is one which emphasises positive working alliances and high expectations for what the young men can achieve in education. Indicators of success include young men reporting:

- a renewed sense of belonging in education;
- increased confidence about their knowledge and learning;
- educators showing an interest in them and their lives;
- feeling more comfortable seeking personal and educational support;

- perceiving learning as being essential for their future opportunities.

2. Demonstrate dignity and respect

Principle 2 sounds simple – when educators are working with young men, it is important that they do so in a way which demonstrates dignity and respect. However, all too often there is an approach to communication, especially with young men who may experience marginalisation, where such demonstrations are notably absent. Instead of communicating to boys that they are inherently valuable, labels such as 'class clown' often achieve the opposite. Research by American academic Lynn Barnett[1] demonstrates just how such notions frame perceptions of their educational identities by teachers as rebellious and intrusive. An understanding which lay in stark contrast to educators' perceptions of girls who, Barnett contends, did not experience the same level of stigmatisation when exhibiting playful behaviour in the classroom. TBS argue that such labels and perceptions need to be challenged. They contend that engagement with young men requires a demonstrable attitude of acceptance and affirmation by educators charged with their care. A powerful, consistent message that they are inherently valuable and worthwhile as unique individuals irrespective of their academic ability. In doing so, the educator avoids belittling, labelling, shaming and stereotyping.

Indicators of success include young men reporting:

- increased self-worth;
- feeling valued in the learning environment;
- enhanced awareness of the importance of the educator's role in their learning journey;
- improved relationships with educators;
- an appreciation and a feeling of mutual respect with educators.

3. Utilise a 'strengths-based approach' to learning

To truly connect with young working-class men in education, this principle argues that we must robustly and intentionally dismantle any notion that they are 'deficient'. While on the surface this may sound like common sense, Chapter 3 which engaged with aspiration demonstrated how, due to wider societal messages, it is all too easy to fall into the trap of framing who the young men are, and where they come from, as a 'problem'. Linked closely with the second principle, it instead calls for educators to adopt an approach which acknowledges the unique strengths that exist within them. Rather than a focus on their perceived deficits, TBS urge educators to tap into the underdeveloped creativity, energy and resources of each boy. While they acknowledge that this can be challenging in educational contexts which, at times, feel designed to achieve the opposite, they argue that doing so is instrumental for young men to maximise their potential.

If achieved, boys will report:

- an appreciation of their abilities beyond academic success;
- increased self-determination, resilience and independence;
- increased awareness and willingness to tap into broader support networks including families, communities and youth services;
- being active as opposed to passive toward setting specific and realistic personal and educational goals;
- increased self-efficacy and feeling more empowered and optimistic about shaping their future.

4. Challenge and affirm masculine identities

Principle 4 resonates not just in education but in a range of settings which constitute the social contexts of the young men we support. Within the stories of my own journey into adulthood, and those from the numerous contributors to this book, we have explored the acute pressure that normative masculine expectations can place on the shoulders of young men. A pressure to behave in a certain way and do certain things. It is a game with no winners. A game in which often young men are either unconscious or unwilling participants. In a world where many teenage boys have turned to TikTok influencers to feel a sense of connection, it is more important than ever that we intentionally challenge and affirm masculine identities in spaces and places of education. However, we need to do so in the right way. Within this principle, TBS state the importance of doing just that.

Linking back to principles 1, 2 and 3, it is the approach we take to doing so, the *how* which is instrumental. Engaging with this principle meaningfully involves a demonstrable appreciation of the internal, often conflicting pressures that young men can experience when constructing their masculine identities. In doing so, educators use the tools at their disposal to engage young men in constructive, open conversations which encourage critical thinking. They challenge narrow and potentially harmful gender stereotypes through meaningful dialogue, intentionally communicating in a way which affirms more positive views and understandings of masculinities.

If educators intentionally apply this principle successfully, boys will report:

- increased awareness of historical, social and cultural attitudes in relation to stereotypes and human behaviour;
- a deeper understanding of why boys, and men, may be reluctant to show certain feelings and emotions or actively seek support;
- being comfortable discussing sensitive and controversial issues not typically addressed in school;
- increased awareness of how traditional notions of men and masculinity can negatively impact societal, community and family attitudes to education and learning;
- learning new skills and discovering alternative ways to manage conflict and better understand expressions of male violence.

5. Promote positive mental health

For reasons that I hope by now are very clear, the next TBS principle carries significant potential. At a time of crisis with the mental health of young people, getting it right facilitates an opportunity to address issues which are particular to boys and young men in a new, more robust manner. Instead of an individualised focus on the mental health of a boy or young man as though it floats free of time, family, place and their relationship with others, principle 5 encourages active engagement with all of those things. By employing this principle, educators will demonstrate an awareness of the multiple and complex pressures which are continually negotiated by young men from areas of social and economic disadvantage. As boys chart their journeys across the turbulent waters of physical, emotional and cognitive development which occur during adolescence, they will benefit from feeling understood. Through easy access to good pastoral care, they will receive encouragement and support to cope better with the stresses and anxieties they encounter.

If implemented successfully, boys will report:

- increased understanding of factors impacting upon their mental and emotional health;
- more self-awareness regarding the source of their own stress triggers, fears and anxieties;
- being more knowledgeable in identifying and availing of educational support and mental health services;
- an increase in confidence, self-esteem and self-image;
- being more resilient and articulating emotional competency.

6. Identify blocks to boys' learning

This principle contends that a significant mechanism to achieve more constructive and meaningful engagement with young men in education is through better identification of their blocks to learning. In *Boys Don't Try? Rethinking Masculinity in Schools*, Pinkett and Roberts go to great lengths to outline how for decades, stereotypical assumptions about what boys 'like' and 'learn best by doing' have dominated perceptions surrounding blocks to learning. Principle 6 suggests that, for work to be more impactful, educators need to abandon such assumptions and actively seek to find out from young men what they perceive these barriers to be. Not as a homogenous group, but as individual learners. TBS state that boys often report feeling overwhelmed once they perceive that they have fallen behind their peers, which leaves them believing they are unable to catch up. If left unaddressed, it can become a self-fulfilling prophecy.[2] Their research demonstrates that boys respond well to tailored, practical solutions that will help them overcome barriers to their learning.

If successfully implemented, boys will demonstrate:

- greater awareness that educational support exists beyond the formal learning environment;
- being less easily distracted and a reduction in disruptive behaviour in the learning environment;
- connecting more with subjects and being more actively engaged in their learning;
- improved attendance and increased self-discipline in setting and completing tasks and meeting deadlines;
- finding learning more relevant, fun and feeling safe and happy in school.

7. Connect boys' learning to context

In the chapters which engaged with the historical legacy of socio-economic inequality for young working-class men, we saw how a complex, ever evolving set of societal conditions influenced and shaped their engagement with education across generations. Yet all too often, alongside issues related to masculinity, it is completely compartmentalised from their learning in the classroom. TBS stress the importance of intentionally working to bridge this divide. By educators seeking to understand the complex social and economic context of each student, learning can be located within their everyday life experience. They argue that this explicit link to their own world helps them better value, appreciate and celebrate their own communities and backgrounds. TBS assert that it also broadens the contextual relevance of learning, making explicit the transformative nature of education.

They contend that this can be achieved through the following:

- making clearer connections between their learning and everyday lives;
- expressing a shift in their attitudes toward education and a belief that they can succeed;
- a stronger desire to set more concrete educational goals;
- awareness of the limitations of certain community traditions and cultural norms;

- relating their life experiences within a broader socio-economic context.

8. Engage meaningfully with boys

Again, the foundational argument which lies at the heart of this principle is that working-class boys are not a homogenous group, and that they will not engage meaningfully in learning until educators engage meaningfully with them. In Chapter 8 which drew on the experiences of the young men who engaged in the Being a Boy project from Seaside Academy, we saw the magic that happened once the young men were introduced to a set of conditions in which they felt safe, seen and heard. This principle recognises that learning is a two-way process. TBS illustrate how, within engaged learning contexts, boys learn from each other, educators learn from boys and boys learn from educators in a reciprocal relationship. Each voice, each experience and each opinion is valued and valuable. The principle recognises the need to find ways for boys to reflect, think, talk and explore issues that are important to them. It involves questioning and frequently seeking feedback, considering the viewpoints of others and encouraging inclusion and diversity.

If educators achieve meaningful engagement, it will be demonstrated through:

- increased confidence in expressing and questioning their thoughts and beliefs;
- less inclination to lose concentration or engage in disruptive behaviour;
- more evidence of depth in their learning;
- valuing the educator as knowledgeable and inspiring;
- a deeper understanding of diverse values, beliefs and life experiences.

9. Enable creative learning environments

At the heart of principle 9 is the notion that learning environments should not be seen by young men as hostile, threatening or judgemental. Instead, TBS research findings have demonstrated that boys thrive in learning environments which are supportive, free from distraction and enjoyable. As highlighted in principles 7 and 8, they learn in a range of different ways in much the same way as educators take different approaches to facilitating learning. They argue that informal educational methodologies have been highly successful at re-engaging boys who have completely disengaged from school-based education. Again, through Being a Boy we engaged a group of young working-class men who fitted this profile precisely. The evidence provided by TBS is backed up by what we experienced first hand. It was demonstrated by reading the poetry that the young men produced, seeing the excited way in which they spoke about exhibiting their photography at home and observing the awkward negotiation of pride on their faces as they celebrated their achievements with their families and friends at an exhibition event.

Indicators of success in the enablement of a creative learning environment include:

• less boredom in the learning environment;
• enjoying learning and having more fun;
• improved relationships with peers and with educators;
• discovering new social and life skills;
• discovering more creative solutions to educational and life challenges.

10. Value the voice of boys

This final principle is emblematic of what we, as educators and wider society, don't do nearly enough of. It involves truly valuing the voices of young working-class men. Listening with deep intentionality. Reflecting on what they are saying, and how it might shape their engagement with the world around them. Basing our practice on learning. Acting only after we've really listened to what young men have to say. Arguably, the effective mobilisation of this principle alone would go a significant way toward countering the unhelpful stereotypes and assumptions about working-class young men which are so often presented as fact. The principle recognises and intentionally promotes the right of boys to fully participate in their own educational journey.

TBS research robustly demonstrates that boys and young men learn more when they are consulted and feel listened to. And when their thoughts, concerns and ideas are positioned as both valued and valuable within the learning environment, they feel that they are too. Indicators of success when attempts are made to intentionally value the voice of boys include:

- the educator demonstrating strong active listening skills;
- the educator treating them more like young adults than boys;
- feeling more confident talking in front of others;
- being respected when sharing their thoughts, concerns and opinions;
- feeling motivated, valued and empowered.

References

Chapter 1

1 GOV.UK (2024) 'Suspensions and permanent exclusions in England, Academic year 2022/23', [online] Available from: https://explore-educat ion-statistics.service.gov.uk/find-statistics/suspensions-and-permanent-exc lusions-in-england/2022-23 [Accessed 17 July 2024].

2 Office for National Statistics (2023) 'Suicides in England and Wales: 2022 registrations', [online] Available from: https://www.ons.gov.uk/peoplepop ulationandcommunity/birthsdeathsandmarriages/deaths/bulletins/suicide sintheunitedkingdom/2022registrations#:~:text=Males%20continued%20 to%20account%20for,rates%20between%202018%20and%202021 [Accessed 17 July 2024].

3 National Alliance to End Homelessness (2019) 'Demographic data project: gender and individual homelessness', [online] Available from: https://endhomelessness.org/demographic-data-project-gender- and-individual-homelessness/#:~:text=Thus%2C%20men%20are%20 the%20majority,first%20installment%20of%20this%20series [Accessed 17 July 2024].

4 HM Prison and Probation Service (2021) 'Offender equalities 2020–21', [online] Available from: https://assets.publishing.service.gov.uk/governm ent/uploads/system/uploads/attachment_data/file/1048255/HMPPS_O ffender_Equalities_2020-21_FINAL_Revision.pdf [Accessed 17 July 2024].

5 Office for Health Improvement and Disparities (2023) 'Substance misuse treatment for adults: statistics 2022 to 2023', [online] Available from: https:// www.gov.uk/government/statistics/substance-misuse-treatment-for-adu lts-statistics-2022-to-2023/adult-substance-misuse-treatment-statistics-2022- to-2023-report [Accessed 17 July 2024].

6 hooks, b. (1994) *Teaching to Transgress: Education as the Practice of Freedom*, New York: Routledge.

7 Crenshaw, K. (2013) 'Demarginalizing the intersection of race and sex: a Black feminist critique of antidiscrimination doctrine, feminist theory and antiracist politics', in K. Maschke (ed) *Feminist Legal Theories*, New York: Routledge, pp 23–51.

8 Butler, J. (2002) *Gender Trouble*, New York: Routledge.

9 Skeggs, B. (2013) *Class, Self, Culture*, London: Routledge.

10 Way, N. (2024) *Rebels with a Cause: Reimagining Boys, Ourselves, and Our Culture*, New York: Penguin Random House.

[11] BBC News (2024) Andrew Tate put under house arrest as new charges emerge, [online] Available from: https://www.bbc.co.uk/news/articles/clyglgy8j3eo [Accessed 23 August 2024].

Chapter 2

[1] Rowling, J.K. (1999) *Harry Potter and the Philosopher's Stone*, London: Bloomsbury.

[2] Naidoo, S. (1972) *Specific Dyslexia: The Research Report of the ICAA Word Blind Centre for Dyslexic Children*, London: Pitman.

[3] History of Dyslexia project (nd) 'A brief history of dyslexia', [online] Available from: https://dyslexiahistory.web.ox.ac.uk/brief-history-dyslexia#:~:text=In%201972%20Naidoo%20published%20Specific,children%2C%20which%20remains%20instructive%20today [Accessed 17 July 2024].

[4] hooks, b. (2005) *The Will to Change: Men, Masculinity, and Love*, New York: Washington Square Press.

[5] Progressive Masculinity (nd) 'About us', [online] Available from: https://www.progressivemasculinity.co.uk/about-us/ [Accessed 2 August 2024].

Chapter 3

[1] Campaign for the Arts (2023) 'Huge decline in arts subjects worsens at GCSE and A level', [online] Available from: https://www.campaignforthearts.org/news/huge-decline-in-arts-subjects-worsens-at-gcse-and-a-level/ [Accessed 28 October 2024].

[2] FFT Education Datalab (2024) 'How has access to creative subjects changed over time?', [online] Available from: https://ffteducationdatalab.org.uk/2024/03/how-has-access-to-creative-subjects-changed-over-time/ [Accessed 28 October 2024].

[3] GOV.UK (nd) 'Widening participation in higher education: 2023', [online] Available from: https://www.gov.uk/government/statistics/widening-participation-in-higher-education-2023 [Accessed 20 October 2024].

[4] British Political Speech (1997) 'General election victory speech, 1997', [online] Available from: http://www.britishpoliticalspeech.org/speech-archive.htm?speech=222 [Accessed 7 August 2024].

[5] The 2010 to 2015 Conservative and Liberal Democrat Coalition government (2011) 'Opening doors, breaking barriers: a strategy for social mobility', [online] p 6, Available from: https://www.gov.uk/government/publications/opening-doors-breaking-barriers-a-strategy-for-social-mobility [Accessed 17 July 2024].

[6] Cameron, D. (2012) 'David Cameron presents himself as leader of "aspiration nation"', *The Guardian*, [online] 10 October, Available from: https://www.theguardian.com/politics/2012/oct/10/david-cameron-leader-aspiration-nation [Accessed 7 August 2024].

[7] Hillman, N. and Robinson, N. (2016) 'Boys to men: the underachievement of young men in higher education – and how to start tackling it', Higher Education

Policy Institute Report 84, [online] Available from: https://www.hepi.ac.uk/wp-content/uploads/2016/05/Boys-to-Men.pdf [Accessed 17 July 2024].

8   Burns, J. (2018) 'Ofsted chief says poor White communities lack "aspiration and drive"', BBC News, [online] Available from: https://www.bbc.co.uk/news/education-44568019 [Accessed 17 July 2024].

9   UCAS (2024) 'UCAS undergraduate end of cycle reports', [online] Available from: https://www.ucas.com/data-and-analysis/undergraduate-statistics-and-reports/ucas-undergraduate-end-cycle-data-resources-2024 [Accessed 21 February 2025].

10 Education Endowment Foundation (nd) 'Aspiration interventions', [online] Available from: https://educationendowmentfoundation.org.uk/education-evidence/teaching-learning-toolkit/aspiration-interventions?utm_source=/education-evidence/teaching-learning-toolkit/aspiration-interventions&utm_medium=search&utm_campaign=site_search&search_term=aspir [Accessed 17 July 2024].

11 Education Endowment Foundation (nd) 'Aspiration interventions', [online] Available from: https://educationendowmentfoundation.org.uk/education-evidence/teaching-learning-toolkit/aspiration-interventions [Accessed 21 February 2025].

12 University of Birmingham (nd) 'Professor David Gillborn', [online] Available from: https://www.birmingham.ac.uk/staff/profiles/education/gillborn-david.aspx [Accessed 17 July 2024].

13 University of Cambridge (nd) 'Diane Reay', [online] Available from: https://www.educ.cam.ac.uk/people/staff/reay/ [Accessed 17 July 2024].

14 University College London (nd) 'Prof Louise Archer', [online] Available from: https://profiles.ucl.ac.uk/61616-louise-archer/publications [Accessed 17 July 2024].

15 Harrison, N. (nd) *Neil Harrison – Educational Research and Commentary*. Available from: https://neil-harrison.me/ [Accessed 21 February 2025].

16 Anon (nd) 'Aspiration', Dictionary.com, [online] Available from: https://www.dictionary.com/browse/aspiration [Accessed 7 August 2024].

17 Blower, A. (2019) 'BTEC vs A-Level', University Toolbox, YouTube, [online] Available from: https://www.youtube.com/watch?v=JFB16smPJSM [Accessed 17 July 2024].

18 Atherton, G. and Mazhari, T. (2019) 'Working-class heroes: understanding access to higher education for White students from lower socio-economic backgrounds', National Education Opportunities Network report.

19 The Week Staff (2021) 'The International Baccalaureate explained', *The Week*, [online] Available from: https://theweek.com/news/education/952208/the-international-baccalaureate-explained [Accessed 17 July 2024].

20 hooks, b. (2014) *Teaching to Transgress: Education as the Practice of Freedom*, New York: Routledge.

21 Freire, P. (1996) *Pedagogy of the Oppressed* (revised edn), New York: Continuum.

22 Harrison, N. and Waller, R. (2018) 'Challenging discourses of aspiration: the role of expectations and attainment in access to higher education', *British Educational Research Journal*, 44(5): 914–38.

23 Cambridge Dictionary (2024) 'Expectation', [online] Available from: https://dictionary.cambridge.org/dictionary/english/expectation#google_vignette [Accessed 1 November 2024].

24 Ball, S.J., Reay, D. and David, M. (2002) '"Ethnic choosing": minority ethnic students, social class and higher education choice', *Race, Ethnicity and Education*, 5(4): 333–57.

25 GOV.UK (2024) 'Key stage 4 performance', [online] Available from: https://explore-education-statistics.service.gov.uk/find-statistics/key-stage-4-performance [Accessed 17 July 2024].

Chapter 4

1 Savage, M. (2015) *Social Class in the 21st Century*, London: Pelican Books.

2 Equality Trust (2024) 'The scale of economic inequality in the UK', [online] Available from: https://equalitytrust.org.uk/scale-economic-inequality-uk/ [Accessed 22 July 2024].

3 Willis, P. (1977) *Learning to Labor: How Working Class Kids Get Working Class Jobs*, New York: Columbia University Press.

4 Willis, P. (1977) *Learning to Labor: How Working Class Kids Get Working Class Jobs*, New York: Columbia University Press, p 13.

5 Willis, P. (2013) *The Ethnographic Imagination*, Hoboken, NJ: John Wiley & Sons, p 86.

6 Brown, P. (2018) *Schooling Ordinary Kids (1987): Inequality, Unemployment, and the New Vocationalism*, Routledge Revivals, London: Routledge.

7 Brown, P. (2018) *Schooling Ordinary Kids (1987): Inequality, Unemployment, and the New Vocationalism, Routledge Revivals*, London: Routledge, p 1.

8 Mac an Ghaill, M. and Haywood, C. (2016) 'Schooling, masculinity and class analysis: towards an aesthetic of subjectivities', in A. Coffey and D. James (eds) *Masculinity and Education*, London: Routledge, pp 144–59.

9 Urban Dictionary (2024) 'Scally', [online] Available from: https://www.urbandictionary.com/define.php?term=Scally [Accessed 1 November 2024].

10 Cambridge Dictionary (2024) 'Chav', [online] Available from: https://dictionary.cambridge.org/dictionary/english/chav [Accessed 28 October 2024].

11 Sveinsson, K.P. (ed) (2009) *Who Cares about the White Working Class?*, London: Runnymede Trust.

12 Ward, M.R.M. (2015) *From Labouring to Learning: Working-Class Masculinities, Education and De-industrialization*, London: Palgrave Macmillan.

13 Alliance of Working-Class Academics (2024) 'Our team', [online] Available from: https://www.workingclassacademics.com/our-team [Accessed 12 August 2024].

14 Roberts, S. (2021) 'A very personal call to action for non-violent men to denounce men's violence', Monash Lens, [online] 28 April, Available from: https://lens.monash.edu/@politics-society/2021/04/28/1383148/a-very-personal-call-to-action-for-non-violent-men-to-denounce-mens-violence [Accessed 12 August 2024].

[15] Monash University (nd) 'Karla Elliott: research outputs', [online] Available from: https://research.monash.edu/en/persons/karla-elliott/publications/ [Accessed 13 August 2024].

Chapter 5

[1] Akala (2019) *Natives: Race and Class in the Ruins of Empire*, London: Two Roads.

[2] Good Morning Britain (2019) 'Rapper Akala on linking knife crime to race', YouTube, [online] Available from: https://www.youtube.com/watch?v= QvS78MlAXAQ&t=65s [Accessed 17 December 2024].

[3] Ruxton, S. and Burrell, S. (nd) 'Now and men: current conversations about men's lives', [online] Available from: https://now-and-men.captivate.fm/ [Accessed 24 August 2024].

[4] Future Men (nd) 'APPG on fatherhood', [online] Available from: https:// futuremen.org/advocacy/appg-on-fatherhood/ [Accessed 13 August 2024].

[5] Future Men (nd) 'Boys development programme', [online] Available from: https://futuremen.org/schools/boys-development-programme/ [Accessed 13 August 2024].

[6] Tarrant, A. (2023) 'Instigating father-inclusive practice interventions with young fathers and multi-agency professionals: the transformative potential of qualitative longitudinal and co-creative methodologies', *Families, Relationships and Societies*, https://doi.org/10.1332/204674321X16913136250482

[7] Brook, O., O'Brien, D. and Taylor, M. (2020) *Culture Is Bad for You: Inequality in the Cultural and Creative Industries*, Manchester: Manchester University Press.

[8] Eddo-Lodge, R. (2020) *Why I'm No Longer Talking to White People about Race*, London: Bloomsbury Publishing.

[9] Warren, J. and Campbell, A. (2023) 'Bianca Williams: two Met officers sacked over athlete search gross misconduct', BBC News, [online] Available from: https://www.bbc.co.uk/news/uk-england-london-67214409 [Accessed 24 August 2024].

[10] Arday, J. (2019) *Cool Britannia and Multi-ethnic Britain: Uncorking the Champagne Supernova*, London: Routledge.

[11] Wallace, D. (2017) 'Reading "race" in Bourdieu? Examining Black cultural capital among Black Caribbean youth in South London', *Sociology*, 51(5): 907–23.

Chapter 6

[1] Adams, M. (2009) 'What Samuel Johnson really did', *Humanities*, 30(5) (September/October), [online] Available from: https://www.neh.gov/hum anities/2009/septemberoctober/feature/what-samuel-johnson-really-did [Accessed 13 August 2024].

[2] Editors of Encyclopaedia Britannica (nd) 'David Garrick', *Encyclopaedia Britannica*, [online] Available from: https://www.britannica.com/biography/ David-Garrick [Accessed 13 August 2024].

[3] Editors of Encyclopaedia Britannica (nd) 'Joseph Addison', *Encyclopaedia Britannica*, [online] Available from: https://www.britannica.com/biography/ Joseph-Addison [Accessed 13 August 2024].

4 Office for Students (nd) 'Young participation by area: search by postcode', [online] Available from: https://www.officeforstudents.org.uk/data-and-analysis/young-participation-by-area/search-by-postcode/ [Accessed 13 August 2024].

5 Department for Education (2023) 'Widening participation in higher education', [online] Available from: https://explore-education-statistics.service.gov.uk/find-statistics/widening-participation-in-higher-education#releaseHeadlines-charts [Accessed 24 August 2024].

6 Pinkett, M. and Roberts, M. (2019) *Boys Don't Try? Rethinking Masculinity in Schools*, London: Routledge.

7 Roberts, M. (2021) *The Boy Question: How to Teach Boys to Succeed in School*, London: Routledge.

8 Jones, S. and Myhill, D. (2004) ' "Troublesome boys" and "compliant girls": gender identity and perceptions of achievement and underachievement', *British Journal of Sociology of Education*, 25(5): 547–61.

9 Jackson, C. (2010) ' "I've been sort of laddish with them … one of the gang": teachers' perceptions of "laddish" boys and how to deal with them', *Gender and Education*, 22(5): 505–19.

10 Jones, S. and Myhill, D. (2004) ' "Troublesome boys" and "compliant girls": gender identity and perceptions of achievement and underachievement', *British Journal of Sociology of Education*, 25(5): 547–61.

11 Barnett, L.A. (2018) 'The education of playful boys: class clowns in the classroom', *Frontiers in Psychology*, 9: article 232.

12 Hamilton, A., Morgan, S., Murphy, B. and Harland, K. (2024) 'Taking Boys Seriously: a participatory action research initiative demonstrating the transformative potential of relational education', *British Journal of Sociology of Education*, 45(2): 284–310.

13 Hamilton, A., Morgan, S., Murphy, B. and Harland, K. (2024) 'Taking Boys Seriously: a participatory action research initiative demonstrating the transformative potential of relational education', *British Journal of Sociology of Education*, 45(2): 296.

Chapter 7

1 MYfs (2023) 'MYTIME Young Carers', [online] Available from: https://www.mytimeyoungcarers.org/ [Accessed 15 August 2024].

2 Children's Society (nd) 'Supporting young carers: facts about young carers', [online] Available from: https://www.childrenssociety.org.uk/what-we-do/our-work/supporting-young-carers/facts-about-young-carers [Accessed 13 August 2024].

3 Carers Trust (nd) 'APPG on young carers and young adult carers: inquiry into life opportunities', [online] Available from: https://carers.org/all-party-parliamentary-group-appg-for-young-carers-and-young-adult-carers/appg-on-young-carers-and-young-adult-carers-inquiry-into-life-opportunities [Accessed 12 August 2024].

4 Joseph, S., Kendall, C., Toher, D., Sempik, J., Holland, J. and Becker, S. (2019) 'Young carers in England: findings from the 2018 BBC survey

on the prevalence and nature of caring among young people', *Child: Care, Health and Development*, 45(4): 606–12.

⁵   Children's Commissioner for England, (2016) 'The support provided to young carers in England', [online] Available from: https://www.childrensc ommissioner.gov.uk/resource/the-support-provided-to-young-carers-in-england/ [Accessed 21 February 2025].

⁶   The Children's Society, 'Supporting young carers', Available from: childrenssociety.org.uk

⁷   Becker, F. and Becker, S. (2008) 'Young adult carers in the UK: experiences, needs and services for carers aged 16–25', pp 16–24 [online] Available from: http://www.youngadultcarers.eu/docs/1738-yac-report-3846.pdf [Accessed 21 February 2025].

Chapter 8

¹   Botto, M. and Gottzén, L. (2024) 'Swallowing and spitting out the red pill: young men, vulnerability, and radicalization pathways in the manosphere', *Journal of Gender Studies*, 33(5): 596–608.

²   Office for Students (2023) 'Access and participation data dashboard', [online] Available from: https://www.officeforstudents.org.uk/data-and-analysis/ access-and-participation-data-dashboard/data-dashboard/ [Accessed 15 August 2024].

³   Arts University Bournemouth (2022) 'Being a Boy 2022 report', [online] Available from: https://webdocs.aub.ac.uk/Being%20a%20Boy%20Imp act%20Report%202022.pdf [Accessed 24 August 2024].

⁴   Department for Education (2023) 'Suspensions and permanent exclusions in England: 2021–22 summer term', [online] Available from: https://expl ore-education-statistics.service.gov.uk/find-statistics/suspensions-and-permanent-exclusions-in-england/2021-22-summer-term [Accessed 24 August 2024].

⁵   Hickson-Lovence, A. (2024) *Wild East* (1st edn), London: Penguin.

⁶   Atta, D. (nd) 'I come from', Into the Outside, [online] Available from: https:// www.intotheoutside.org.uk/voices/dean-atta/i-come-from/ [Accessed 16 August 2024].

⁷   Robb, M. (2021) ' "Men, we just deal with it differently": researching sensitive issues with young men', *International Journal of Social Research Methodology*, 24(5): 617–25.

⁸   Open University (2024) 'Jon Rainford: Open research', [online] Available from: https://research.open.ac.uk/people/jr24883 [Accessed 16 August 2024].

⁹   Blower, A. and Rainford, J. (2023) 'Internalizing the present in the articulation of the future: masculinity, inequality, and trying on new possible selves', *Boyhood Studies*, 16(2): 109–32.

¹⁰ Rainford, J. (2023) 'Are we still "raising aspirations"? The complex relationship between aspiration and widening participation practices in English higher education institutions', *Educational Review*, 75(3): 411–28.

[11] Markus, H. and Nurius, P. (1986) 'Possible selves', *American Psychologist*, 41(9): 954–69.

[12] Henderson, H. (2018) 'Borrowed time: a sociological theorisation of possible selves and educational subjectivities', in H. Henderson, J. Stevenson and A.-M. Bathmaker (eds) *Possible Selves and Higher Education*, London: Routledge, pp 27–40.

[13] Harrison, N. (2018) 'Using the lens of "possible selves" to explore access to higher education: a new conceptual model for practice, policy, and research', *Social Sciences*, 7, 209(10): 1–21.

[14] hooks, b. (1994) *Teaching to Transgress: Education as the Practice of Freedom*, New York: Routledge.

[15] Freire, P. (1996) *Pedagogy of the Oppressed* (revised edn), New York: Continuum.

[16] Giroux, H.A. (2011) *On Critical Pedagogy*, New York: Continuum.

[17] Hickson-Lovence, A. (2020) *The 392*, OWN IT! Publishing.

Chapter 9

[1] Ulster University (nd) 'Taking Boys Seriously', [online] Available from: https://www.ulster.ac.uk/research/topic/social-work-and-social-pol icy/research-themes/taking-boys-seriously [Accessed 24 August 2024].

[2] Harland, K. and McCready, S. (2012) 'Taking Boys Seriously: a longitudinal study of adolescent male school life experiences in Northern Ireland', Ulster University, Available from: https://pure.ulster.ac.uk/ws/portalfiles/portal/11350226/Taking_Boys_Seriously_DE_FINAL_PDF.pdf [Accessed 20 October 2024].

[3] Hamilton, A., Morgan, S., Murphy, B. and Harland, K. (2024) 'Taking Boys Seriously: utilising participatory action research to tackle compounded educational disadvantage', *Action Research*, 0(0).

[4] Taking Boys Seriously (TBS) Research (2023) 'TBS Monkstown Boxing Club', YouTube, [online] Available from: https://www.youtube.com/watch?v=XRfjnp4xRUk [Accessed 30 October 2024].

[5] TBS Research (2023) 'TBS Holy Family YC', YouTube, [online] Available from: https://www.youtube.com/watch?v=JQsVspo-ASY [Accessed 30 October 2024].

[6] TBS Research (2023) 'TBS Abbey Community College Mr. Smyth', YouTube, [online] Available from: https://www.youtube.com/watch?v=fUqfXX82Qk8 [Accessed 30 October 2024].

[7] Ulster University (nd) 'UU TBS principles', [online] Available from: https://www.ulster.ac.uk/__data/assets/pdf_file/0016/1511242/UU-TBS-Princip les.pdf [Accessed 19 December 2024].

[8] Arts University Bournemouth (2023) 'Dorset Boys Impact hub', [online] Available from: https://aub.ac.uk/schools-hub/dorset-boys-impact-hub [Accessed 19 December 2024].

[9] Bournemouth University Podcast (2024) 'Valuing the voice of boys', Spotify, [online] Available from: https://open.spotify.com/episode/4LvNnhH862k 5tGFjuT3iGS [Accessed 21 August 2024].

[10] Boys' Impact (2024) 'Boys' Impact', Available from: https://www.boysimp act.com/ [Accessed 13 August 2024].

[11] Chartered College of Teaching (nd) 'Chartered College of Teaching', Available from: https://chartered.college/ [Accessed 21 August 2024].

Conclusion

[1] Bola, J.J. (2019) *Mask Off: Masculinity Redefined* (1st edn), London: Pluto Press, p 8.

[2] Channel 4 (2024) *Danny Dyer: How to Be a Man*, [online] Available from: https://www.channel4.com/programmes/danny-dyer-how-to-be-a-man [Accessed 23 August 2024].

[3] Leszkiewicz, A. (2024) 'Teenage boys talk masculinity in About the Boys on Radio 4', *New Statesman*, [online] Available from: https://www.newst atesman.com/culture/radio-podcasts/2024/04/teenage-boys-talk-masculin ity-about-the-boys-radio-4 [Accessed 21 August 2024].

[4] UK Parliament (2024) 'General election 2024: Select Committees', [online] Available from: https://committees.parliament.uk/committee/203/educat ion-committee/news/201773/general-election-2024-select-committees/ [Accessed 21 August 2024].

[5] hooks, b. (2005) *The Will to Change: Men, Masculinity, and Love*, New York: Washington Square Press, p 54.

Appendix

[1] Barnett, L.A. (2018) 'The education of playful boys: Class clowns in the classroom', *Frontiers in Psychology*, (9): 232.

[2] Rist, R. (1970) 'Student social class and teacher expectations: The self-fulfilling prophecy in ghetto education', *Harvard Educational Review*, 40(3): 411-51.

Index

'AB' refers to the author. 'TBS' refers to the Taking Boys Seriously initiative. Pseudonyms are indicated by ⋆.